SAVAGE RECOVERY

SAVAGE RECOVERY

△MANI P.

HOW A PACIFIC ISLAND KID GOES FROM A MAJOR DRUG DEALER
TO FEDERAL PRISON TO RECOVERY AND
HEALING THE EMOTIONAL TRAUMA FROM HIS CHILDHOOD

All rights reserved. No part of this book may be reproduced by any mechanical, photographic, or electronic process, or in the form of a phonographic recording, nor may it be stored in a retrieval system, transmitted, or otherwise be copied for public or private use – other than for "fair use" as brief quotations embodied in articles and reviews – without prior written permission of the author.

The author does not dispense medical advice or prescribe the use of any technique as a form of treatment for physical, emotional, or medical problems without the advice of a physician, either directly or indirectly. The intent of the author is only to offer information of a general nature to help you in your journey into sobriety and emotional well-being. In the event that you use any of the information in this book for yourself, the author and publisher assume no responsibility for your actions.

Various print and internet sources of The Big Book and the King James Version of the Holy Bible were used in the writing and editing of this book.

Copyright ©2023 by Manisela Vincent Prescott
ISBN 979-8-218-26371-3

To contact the author, email: prescottmanisela@gmail.com
To contact the editor, @LoveNeenaLove on all social media platforms.

Publishing & Cover Design: 2FeetPro.com
Photo credits:
Plato Terentey. Mike Bird. Pavel Danilyuk. Pixabay. Alex Conchillos.
Cover fonts:
Universal Serif. Bebas. Arial.

www.2FeetPro.com

HAWAII | SOUTH CAROLINA

ACKNOWLEDGEMENTS

I want to thank my mom who passed during my struggles. We often put so much stress, hurt, and heartache on those who love us most. My mom was always fighting for my time and attention, which as alcoholics/addicts, we have none to spare. My mom said, "Your greatest achievement in life I can remember you by is your recovery. It's not exactly like being drafted to the NFL or graduating college even but I'll take it." I LOVE YOU always, Mom! Oh, how I miss you. Eight years clean and sober.

I want to thank my criminal defense lawyer/sponsor, Erik B. who 12-stepped me in jail. This guy would go on to quit practicing criminal law to do personal injury and win the biggest case in United States history against human trafficking. He was the first lawyer to file a lawsuit against internet giant backpage.com and win. His representation of the minors who were pimped on that website has been documented in the film, I Am Jane Doe.

He is a recovery evangelist who my creator had put in the right place, at the right position to deliver me the message of recovery. He is one of the humblest and most loving human beings I know. He is known in the streets as my Dad.

I want to thank my friend and sobriety brother House, who has been there throughout my journey. Me him, and Jesh were known as House, condo, and apartment because we were sobriety brothers who went to a ton of meetings together. He is an inspiration and motivation for my climb.

I want to thank the "opps" or haters who believed that I would fail without them. God will use the most unlikely people to minister that His glory may be fulfilled. Thank you for dropping me that I would find that drive and motivation to find those strangers who played a huge role in my success.

And lastly, thank you to the editor/publisher Neena Love who has been a family friend from young. Thank you for the support and belief when I started writing from prison on a smart phone.

God bless you and keep you.

This book is dedicated to my sobriety brother,
Jeshua Myron,
whom I've lost along my journey to recovery.

My sobriety brother, House,
who celebrated 20 years of clean time,
proving we do recover.

My Mom, who cheered me on
when I found my sobriety.

My children, who I've lost during
my battle against my addiction.

And my Creator, whom without, I'd be nothing.
Never allowing me to stay comfortably in defeat.

INTRODUCTION

I assume if you picked up this book you are either interested in recovery, in recovery, or know someone that can use this recovery book. I wrote this book about overcoming the overwhelming challenges and barriers in my life while working the 12-Step program. I've faced a lot of adversity and trials in "trying to change" and I hope that my experience, strength, and hope can help someone facing similar struggles achieve my same success. I was told by my sponsor (my criminal defense attorney before I sobered up, becoming his sponsee) that there are certain people that only those in similar situations can reach. I believe this. It takes one to know one.

In this book are many of my experiences and wisdom from interactions and conversations with elders in the recovery community. There are sayings that are inspiring, motivating, and uplifting. Things you wouldn't hear anywhere else in the world except a recovery meeting. Within these pages are a lot of humorous wit and tragic events that helped me break through barriers I've subconsciously built that kept me mentally, emotionally, and spiritually blocked, which stunted my growth and development. I pray you find my experience and strength as a gift to embrace in battling whatever you are going through. I pray you find something in the pages that will boost your courage to make your life work for you. If not, I promise you, at the least, this book will entertain the heck out of you.

SAVAGE POLITICS

Proverbs 19:21
Many plans are in a man's heart but
the Lord's purpose will prevail.

CHAPTER ONE

"IN A WORLD OF CHAOS, THE ONLY CONSTANT IS CHANGE," is a quote I've been reading every day for the last two years while living in the SHU. The SHU (Segregation Housing Unit) or "the Hole" as it's known to prison inmates, is solitary confinement. A prison inside of prison. A Hell inside of Hell. It is the epicenter of the black hole in a dark empty universe where inmates are isolated in the middle of nowhere. And yet, this is where I've chosen and managed to spend most of my years while incarcerated – in the SHU – consorting and bonding with other troublesome inmates who were always fighting, gambling, or disobeying the laws of the land, when they were out in the general population.

I had been in and out of the SHU for everything from fighting, assault on an officer, investigation for ordering a stabbing of another inmate, to stabbing another inmate. Today, I've been here for two years straight because of a hostile takeover, prison riot in Cedar Creek Correctional Facility in Little Rock, Washington. A riot that involved attacking the warden and taking over the prison. This incident earned me a First-Degree Prison Rioting charge to add to the lengthy rap sheet of charges I already had. This incident, which solidified my infamy and stupidity in the Washington state prison world could have been prevented, I believe, had the warden done his job.

The riot, which had been brewing over staff targeting me, had finally kicked off when they plucked my last straw. The staff had asked me to clean up poop that someone splashed in their duty office. The messed-up thing was that the staff that were doing the targeting were islanders. Them, along with their hillbilly counterparts, were the kind of people that look down on us for being in prison. The islander staff would often make remarks like, "It's Samoans like you that gives us a bad name," and yada yada yada. When I argued that I wasn't trained in HAZMAT, the officers responded that the poop wouldn't kill me. I complained that I worked in the kitchen and that they have unit porters to clean the units.

They retorted, "You are going to clean this because we're telling you to."

After relentlessly trying to plead my case, which they weren't hearing at all, I stated politely, "I know you guys are trying to mess with me because I have a reputation for being troublesome. So kindly, if you guys would leave me alone, I promise I won't break your jaws if you call me on the P.A. system again to clean this mess. Okay?"

Then I walked off.

And as I was walking back to my bunk, they called over the P.A. system telling me to clean the poop. NOW!!! I calmly took two fire extinguishers off the wall after lighting a cigarette (smoking was not allowed in state prisons at the time of course) and walked back to the officer duty station armed for battle. I threw one of the fire extinguishers through the window of the staff duty station while they were all inside laughing. In the court documents they said that one staff member was injured really bad and that the fire extinguisher almost hit another in the head. But it's all politics. None of the guards sustained any real injuries but they had to make it look good.

I threw the fire extinguisher so hard it launched like a torpedo through the office window leaving a huge hole in the center. What can I say? I then proceeded to take the other fire extinguisher and stick the hose inside the huge hole and sprayed the officers. Not so funny then because they stopped laughing. The truth is, they saw me walking up to the duty station with the fire extinguishers and burning cigarette. They were scrambling to get out through the backdoor while one officer stood there stunned, continuing to get sprayed.

I reached in through the hole, grabbed the phone that was linked to the P.A. system and made an announcement. "This is your new warden speaking, please evacuate the building as my new staff is going to be burning down the place," and before I could tell the other islanders to burn the place down the place was already engulfed in flames.

The quote, etched out from the paint on the door, intrigued me because it is like a brain teaser. *In a world of chaos, the only constant is change.* You could drive yourself nuts trying to figure it out. It's like some kind of philosophical BS that some random joe, dying of boredom, would post online. Or some random joe, literally dying of boredom here, had carved into the door. It was probably some random guy parroting wisdom he heard. But for whatever strange reason it was quoted, it was deep enough to spark questions in me.

So much so it piqued my philosophical interest and left me uneasy and bugged me every day for the last two years.

In the SHU, there's a "yellow" line that is painted on the floor near the door. If you want to go to the yard, you must be up and standing on this line by 5:30 a.m. You must be naked with your pumpkin orange jumpsuit and underwear in your hand ready to be handed out through the tray slot so the staff can search it for contraband while watching you through the window in the door. The search is routine for security measures.

Stretch your arms straight out while doing the spirit fingers.

Run your fingers through your hair.

Show me the back of your ears.

Open your mouth wide exposing the insides.

Lift up your junk.

Turn around and show me the bottom of your feet, one at a time, each time wiggling your toes.

Squat down, spread 'em, and give two good coughs.

When they assess that you do not pose a danger, they will hand you your clothes back and you can get dressed and cuffed up (let them put handcuffs and shackles on you) so you can be transported to the yard area. Everywhere you go in the SHU, you are handcuffed and shackled.

If you are hungry, you better be on that yellow line come breakfast, lunch, or dinner because they will wheeze on by you leaving you starving and waiting for the next meal. I'm usually up way before the meal cart arrives trying to get my daily 500 push up count before bed and I've already lost 30 pounds on this involuntary diet. Every day: Up, down, up, down, reading the etched quote. *IN A WORLD OF CHAOS, THE ONLY CONSTANT IS CHANGE.*

In the 18th century, the SHU, or solitary confinement, was first experimented with in the Eastern State Penitentiary in Philadelphia. It was said that the Quaker Group (Benjamin Franklin, Benjamin Rush, and others), some of whom were founding fathers of our nation, believed that prisoners isolated in stone cold cells with only a Bible would use the time to repent and find spirituality. Consequently, many of the inmates went crazy and couldn't adapt to society when let out, so the practice was slowly done away with. However, because prisons have become popularly a lucrative business in the United States recently, the profiteers who built the prisons across the U.S. built every one of them with the SHU intact, hoping they can succeed where the founding fathers failed.

The profiteers who built the new solitary confinement built it with the psychology in mind that they could improve on the old method by now incorporating generic mandatory rehabilitation programs to educate inmates on behavior modification benefits. One of the privileges for learning about behavior modification was extended visiting hours. They used extra visiting hours as an incentive to try and attract inmates who had families driving from far away towns. Coincidentally, that is 99.9% of the prison population because prisons are commonly built in some Schitt's Creek backwoods far, far away, and its occupants are mainly inner-city kids from impoverished backgrounds. Impoverished families do not have the resources to make the trek out to Schitt's Creek backwoods.

The profiteers believe that their method would be similar to putting a child in a corner and then offering them an explanation as to why they were put in time out. To encourage the child to keep from misbehaving they allowed him to play with friends (visitors), like there's a huge difference between the implementation strategies they used than that of the founding fathers. Well, let me tell you something, solitary confinement is not a good rehabilitation method for humans. The corners of a home are far different from the dark corners of a cement cell in freezing cold temperatures with a thin blanket for warmth and a Bible for a pillow. Studies have shown that long periods of time in solitary confinement has led to anxiety, severe depression, and suicide. If you ever spent time in solitary confinement, you can hear kicking doors and screaming from cells where guys are losing their minds regularly and daily.

If the prison systems worked at rehabilitating anyone, then why is the number of incarcerated persons in America drastically rising instead of declining? Why does America have the highest incarceration rate of persons per country around the world? And why did it take so long for anyone to finally come out about the systemic racism targeting certain impoverished areas of the country filled with minorities, to occupy these new prisons?

With all these generic programs the profiteers implemented, none of it ever was proven to work. There is no data or statistical study to prove that these programs have ever effectively kept a guy from wanting to come back to the SHU or prison. They have offered programs like the Step-Down Program where an inmate would have to denounce his gang affiliation and/or debrief and disclose gang secrets. That inmate, working his way back into the general population, would be targeted and attacked by his former gang the minute he is let out, for having joined such a ridiculous program. It's a death trap. Other similar programs such as the Legacy and Integrity program have similar failure rates. In truth, these programs seem like just another avenue in which the state or federal prisons use to request more funding from the Federal Government. The only programs that boast any real success rates are the ones founded by inmates, which are most likely not supported by the state and feds and are strongly discouraged.

I'm not belittling these programs that do have little success rates. I just feel that the programs offered are satisfied with the minimal success they have and because of it, they don't push to improve. It's the "well-we-saved-one-life" mentality that is troubling to me. Reason being is that compliance is all that is required to pass, and compliance is nothing more than minimum participation. I knew guys that were facilitating the programs that would tell others to join just to make it look good on paper. Same inmates were being forced to falsify the numbers of attendees when program numbers dwindled.

CHAPTER TWO

Well, with all the trouble the founding fathers went through trying to help man find God, discipline, and change, they are going to be sorely disappointed to find out what we have brewing in the works today. Today, we are going to prove to the profiteers why their generic methods of rehabilitation do not work. We are going to show them how keeping us in the SHU for two years resulted in a maladaptive growth, rather than a spiritual one, and how dangerous we can be when we want to be. Today we are going to execute a prison attack on a prison guard, and we are going to do it all from right here in their solitary confinement. This is what happens when the belly of the beast starts grumbling and becomes upset, and this particular guard knows just how to stir things up.

They say rehabilitation is defined as taking a person out of their environment, fixing them, and returning them to their natural environment better than before. The thing is, some of our natural environments have an influential impact on us far greater than we can withstand. No matter how much the prisons change us, a breath of fresh air surrounded by the wrong people in our natural environments can change us right back.

To restore the criminally broken to a state that is far better than they found them, requires a tremendous amount of hard work. Work that the profiteers don't want to pay for because mental health expenses are a costly budget, but it's what I believe will effectively change the system. Psychology and recovery. They do have MRT groups but Moral Recognitive Therapy through a textbook is not effective therapy, despite what they believe. The people in the SHU, people like me, usually are the sick-and-crazy, above-the law, can't-stop-themselves, can't-adapt-to-society types. We are not bad people that need to be good. We are sick people that need to get well. We don't need to be punished. We need to be treated. Everyone in the SHU has addict-like behavior that makes us prone to easily become addicted to something or susceptible to violence if we don't get it. This is a sickness that is treatable through recovery and therapy. Not through some "Do It Yourself" booklet. A broken brain can't fix a broken brain no matter how many psychotherapy books you throw at it.

Prisons, to me, always seemed like the hospitals for the spiritually sick, with the SHU being its insane asylum. The easiest way to describe a prison is the Walking Dead television series. There are a bunch of walking dead zombies just wandering about in the general population, aimlessly, where there's only a few survivors left. The survivors band together in groups and try to isolate themselves from these airheads just roaming about as if they are sleepwalking. The walkers are those that are shunned and looked at degradingly by the survivors. Rapists, pedophiles, weirdos, average joes and such are categorized as walkers. They are soft targets and taken advantage of frequently. Some are not really hardened criminals. They are hardened weirdos. They go in and out of the system continuously because they can't seem to break free from the cycle once they begin. There is a huge difference in prison between a walker and a survivor. Inmate and convict. Being shunned and being respected. An inmate – or walker – will walk into a situation where a guy is getting attacked and just sit there and watch. Thus, making himself a witness or target for no reason. Whereas a convict – or survivor – will walk right by a situation paying no mind to it. If it doesn't involve his friends or himself, it's not his business. Sometimes, you can watch a prison crowd move and tell who the walking dead are, and who are the survivors because a walker will bump into a survivor absentmindedly and get himself stabbed in the head. Now saying that nonchalantly should tell you how prison has affected my mental health.

    I truly believe prisons molded some of us recovering drunks to be the best survivors in life because I have seen a lot of survivors get out and adapt to any situation or change. I have known of many who are successful in their careers and home life. Regardless of how many of people return to prison, statistically based on the 70% of the inmate population that will come back within only a two-year period of being out, the chances of a survivor returning is slim. They do possess sociopathic traits and sometimes have no regard for the law and consequences, doing the necessary evil to survive outside, so there are some that return. But not many. To prove my point that survivors fare well in situations, I had a cell phone in my prison during the COVID epidemic. I started a food blog of dishes and desserts I created. Dishes that made people's mouth's water like I was a chef at a five-star restaurant. Fancy cheesecakes and blueberry pies made of lemon juice and creamers. I showed the world that the prison morale was positive and hopeful even though prisoners were aware that the prisons were having outbreaks across the country. Meanwhile, the U.S. was on a two-week isolation and ordinary people were letting the squirrels in their head drive them nuts, so much that the suicide rates spiked upwards nationwide. We prisoners were confined to a wing in our units in prison.

I call prison a hospital for the spiritually sick because growing up I was taught prison was the opposite of a church. But it's worse than a hospital. It's a dang concrete cemetery with numbered doors like its marked graves, with souls buried alive inside, awaiting a resurrection. I was always made to believe this is where the wicked atoned for their sins with time. It was like, if you don't go to church, you're going to end up in prison.

A lot of the walking dead, you would be surprised, are well educated and very intelligent. These guys are actually educated dummies that can explain psychology, anthropology, sociology, technology, astronomy and whatever else-ology; but don't know what to do to save their own lives in the midst of an economic collapse, an animal attack, a flat tire or even worse, a zombie apocalypse breakout. These types aren't entirely hopeless in prison though because I've seen some of them get out and use what they've learned to get rich and become successful. Legitimate or not.

Every prison across America is usually the same. It is commonly built in some backwoods remote location where some hillbilly inbred from Schitt's Creek is hired to work. Prisons pretty much operate the same way everywhere. Operations are typically standardized nationwide. In the SHU however, things are entirely different depending on staff. You are stripped of all your privileges and are pretty much sitting in a cell for 24-hours a day at the mercy of the inbred guards on shift. If you are lucky, you get 23 hours in your cell and are let out for one hour of recreation time. This is probably the only privilege you have left to enjoy while down here.

Many men look forward to this single hour out because they can be outside basking in the sun even though they are caged in a tiny yard area. This area is usually as small as a dog kennel, or a glass box room and it is fixed with fences all around you. I don't know why they put the fences on the ceilings, like we would somehow figure a way to steal the stars and sky, had the fences not been there. But hey, some mental genius designed this place with layering fences over fences, and razors over razors. I'm just lucky if I can get one hour out when I do. No complaints.

On this particular day though, the staff we're targeting, a hillbilly Schitt's Creek corn fed High School dropout of a guard, decides he is going to burn us (deprived us) out of our yard. He blames it on being short staffed. He also condemns us for being bad stating, "If you didn't come to prison in the first place you wouldn't be beggin' to see the sun now, wouldya?" He decided that not only is he taking our yard privileges, but decides why not push the envelope further. Why not burn us out of our dinners too, right? There's nothing we can do about it. He walks right by our doors while we are standing there looking famished and silly right on the yellow line. To add insult to injury, from our windows in our cells, we could see him in the officer station eating our meals.

These types of people feel it's their job to punish the inmates, not considering that being sent to prison by the courts was punishment enough. He doesn't consider the fact that we have families who have to endure our every struggle and suffering we go through, worrying when we don't eat or write. Every time he's on shift it's the same thing with him. The inmates are tired of this and want to teach him a lesson he'll never forget. If they think two years in this hell hole will fix our bad behavior, then they got something else coming because one thing about prisoners you should know is, they know all about their rights but don't know a dang thing about their wrongs.

CHAPTER THREE

Eating our dinners and starving us out caused a commotion amongst the inmates which caused the plan to be hatched. It's the staff's world, they believe, and they can do whatever they want to inmates and think no one will do anything about it. But we're not just your average inmates. We live in the basement of this spiritual hospital for a reason. We are the worst kind of sick – the kind that will hurt themselves just to hurt you to get revenge. The kind that what will sink to the lowest of lows to exact their revenge on you. The kind of sick that there is no cure for.

This is our home. Our territory. We know every routine minute by minute. We know the exact number of steps from our rooms to the next, all the way down to the shower and yard. We know the mechanics of the prison and how it operates. Since the SHU usually has no supervision or oversight for this kind of staff behavior, they typically get away with it. But we survivors feel it's our duty to regulate this behavior and stop this from happening to us or anyone again. The sad thing about the SHU is that most of the guards who get in trouble for some bad behavior in the general population get sent to work here. And this particular staff we are attacking has had his fill with being a problematic jerk in GP. To say crap trickles down hill is an understatement because we also get the butt end of it all.

Before I go on, I have to explain that in the SHU, there are Protective Custody cases here. Inmates that are afraid for their lives and are housed here for their own protection. Usually sex offenders or snitches or, sometimes, just scaredy cats. Then there's guys like me – the fighters, the gamblers, the rioters and so on. Because of this reason, secret communications are necessary and vital to the success of our secret planned covert mission because rapists, snitches, and scaredy cats are never included in our reindeer games. The "Green River Killer," Gary Ridgeway was amongst one of those inmates housed in this SHU after I left. Robert Yates the Spokane Serial killer is another amongst the Protective custody cases and lives a few doors down from me. The most troubling thing to me about these guys, is that every day, during mail calls, these weirdos get tons of marriage proposals and money orders sent in by women and men strangers. The staff would have to literally open their cuff ports just to pour their mail in because they would have stacks of it. Most of us are stressed hoping to get a letter from our girlfriends or loved ones just to feel alive. Meanwhile, these weirdos are being supported and taken care of by strangers. I'll never understand the fascination of it all, but down here they are just another numbered door with a sick spirit inside.

The plan is simple, and the inmates have coordinated their plan of attack through communicating through the vents and toilets. Some things that are too sensitive to yell through the wire, we have taken the risk of writing on toilet paper and "fishing" over to each other. Fishing is sliding an issued bob parker comb with a string from our clothes tied to one end, with the note attached to it. This can be slid under each other's doors from the next room or from down the hall. We can slide this fishing rod out and the intended recipient will do the same. When our wires tangle, he can then pull the line into his house and read the note. Since I speak four languages, I am designated as the communications coordinator for this, said, simple plan to work. The same poop bomber from the riot who blew up the staff office and caused the staff to target me for cleaning, is with us in the SHU from the riot incident. He plays a vital role in our plan of attack. We've designated him to be the bomber with one other bomber on standby.

THE PLAN

STEP ONE: The bomber brews up what's called a 'poop bomb.' It is a concoction of poop mixed with water in a cup. When the staff opens the cuff port (a metal slot in the door for sliding trays in to feed the inmates) the shUNI bomber will pretend to reach out for the tray but instead grab the guard's hand and pull him down, while with his other hand stick the bomb out and splash the lazy punk in the face with the surprise attack. When this happens, all the other inmates in participation will proceed in unison to flood their cells. By the time the guards shut off the water supply in realization that there's a Wild Waves theme park in the unit, we will have moved on to step two.

STEP TWO: Cover the cell windows with wet toilet paper. In the SHU, it doesn't matter what prison you are at in the United States of America. If an inmate covers his window, for security purposes, the staff MUST remove it to be able to see the inmate. If not, this is a safety hazard not just for the inmates, but for staff alike. If an inmate refuses when the staff asks him to take the covering down, then the staff will have to suit up and request the help of a team of goon squad staffers armed with a riot shield to take the coverings off personally.

Distressingly for the prisons, getting the goon squad requires the prisons to then get other staff members to leave their posts and come join in the fight at the good old SHU. This could halt prison operations especially if they're already understaffed, which most likely they are. Or at least according to the targeted staff they are. Once they get their goon squad suited up and ready, they come in a single file formation with the first staff holding a riot shield in front of him or her. The way things normally work is, they would try to gas the inmate out first. The way the gassing works is, they stick a canister of oleoresin capsicum (OC) aerosol dispenser in the tray slot, and spray you full of gas. This would be in the hopes that the inmate surrenders after suffocating from the gas inhalation and disorientation. But if you are determined to give them hell though, then pepper spray or gas won't hurt you any. It's a small price to pay for the execution of the big plan. Gassing inmates is much like spraying staff with the fire extinguishers except worse.

I bet some of you have watched TV shows and seen peaceful negotiations between the guards and inmates. That's what they display on shows like Lock Up. They only show the things that depict their cordial and peaceful tactics. They don't show how cruel and vicious these cops can really be and that's to avoid risking a major lawsuit for cruel and unusual punishment of inmates. I can guarantee you that if you have made it thus far, to where they must suit up and get the goon squad, you are going to be punished severely for it.

And it's not cordially done like you see on TV at all, where they are talking to the inmate. TV is all a song-and-dance, pony show for the public and is phony as heck.

In real life, once they've sprayed the inmate, they open his cell and then rush in to subdue him physically with restraints and take the coverings off the window. Inmates are jumped on and pinned to the ground with a few kicks and punches to the face and body. Afterwards, they'd go about their business like it was just another day at the office. The inmate who was misbehaving is taken to a tiny cell called isolation where he is stripped naked and left there for three to five days handcuffed to a single metal stool in the center of the floor (until he gets his act together). Remember that the SHU is freezing cold and is sometimes called the "morgue" because of its freezing temperature so being naked in isolation is pure torturous Hell.

STEP FOUR: This is the utmost important of all steps. Stick to the script and see it through. Give them hell when they enter your battlefield, which is your tiny cell you've prepared for a counteroffensive. This is the most critical of all steps considering you have followed the steps in order.

I know… you must be thinking, well, whatever happened to STEP THREE? Well, that's the thing. Step three almost always fails in prison plans. Let me tell you why. Plans usually go awry when you don't consider everything and especially if you don't follow the plan as instructed. This is how it went awry for us on this cold wet and dark day. In life, things don't always go according to plan, and I learned that the hard way on that day, like on many days in my life, because I don't always plan for everything like an educated dummy. But this one was the most memorable experience of all because it left me shell shocked. Literally. So, pay close attention.

CHAPTER FOUR

On D-Day: The guard hands the tray to the bomber and is met with surprise. The poop bomb exploded beautifully. Waterfalls started streaming out of the cells of the inmates who were participating. All the inmates start kicking their doors, screaming the cries of victory. The Goon squad comes in and the first house they go to is mine. They figured it out through confidential sources or just plain common sense that I'm the ringleader in this whole mess. They figured if they could get me to succumb to their terms that the others would follow suit. I had my bed rolled tied with sheets which is what inmates use as shields. My face is covered by my wet t-shirt like a ninja mask which is what's supposed to be technically STEP THREE. Shield your face from gas. Use your bed shield as protection against the shield, and no matter what happens, DO NOT abandon your shields. It's all you have. Fight on!

I'm sticking to the plan and taunting them with all

the bad words I could get out. I'm like a demon-possessed raving lunatic. They gas me but it's a small thing to a giant. I'm screaming for more. Begging for it. I refuse to back down and play their pony in the song and dance show. I'm still jumping for joy all around my flooded, gassed cell. I can hear the cheers from my fellow inmates and the loud kicking on the doors for moral support. The guards finally open my door, and they rush in like a defensive tackle line with everyone behind the first guy carrying the shock shield. Where I screwed up was, for the life of me, I did the educated dummy move. I abandoned my shield and improvised step three in the midst of battle, hoping to gain the upper hand advantage by jumping on them first.

The door cracks open. I abandoned my bed shield and rushed forward. The first guy with the shock shield shocks me and I go down. Timmmmmbbeerrrr!!! I didn't know about the shock shields until then. Like I said, I was shell shocked, no pun intended. I dropped to my back like a quarterback sacked, laid out on the floor in about four inches of water. The first guy falls on me. The entire team does a six-man pile up on him. All the while the shock shield is jolting me with 50,000 volts flowing through it mounted on my chest. I'm lying in water, and I can feel myself painfully separating like my spirit was trying to leave my body. I, all of a sudden, was watching myself standing over my body trying to tell them to get off him, meaning me.

Before I exited my body, all I can remember is the first guy with the shield in between us. I'm looking at his angry face through the plexiglass shield and I can't bring myself to scream or utter a single sound. No one told me that the shields were armed with electricity racing back and forth on the front end, and that this surge of electricity would shoot right through me like a lightning bolt coursing through my veins, locking up every muscle in my body. This made me a complete statue under this human pyramid of guards with the spasms of electric shock. I could smell burning like someone was cooking human flesh. I regretted my decision to get on this wild wave ride, but it was too late, there was no going back now.

They had me squished to the floor thinner than Sunday prison pancakes, and all I could do to cry was formulate a tear that would not drop but hang out on the corner of my eye. It was like that one tear was just loitering on the street corner of my face. Every muscle was shocked stiff. I found myself under this human pyramid feeling like I was getting electrocuted with the worst bladder infection ever, times ten. I'd finally sailed Schitt's creek raging rivers with no paddles and had gotten more rage than I bargained for.

My muscles and everything were so constricted that even weeks after the incident my body would twitch with spasms. Still, to this day, I am easily shocked by electrostatics from just taking clothes out the dryer, or just someone touching my hand. I'm telling you, if you have never been shocked to where you feel you are suspended in time, and you can watch your life pass before your eyes like you're on your social media feed scrolling in rapid flipping motion, with each passing post being an important life's events flying by – trust me, you don't want to try this. I had been jumped by a rival gang and left for dead. Shot by a rival gang and left for dead. Stabbed in prison during a gang fight and none of it was as bad as this incident. It just never occurred to me that *"In a world of chaos, the only constant is CHANGE,"* and that if I wasn't willing to change, then chaos would be the price I paid for living.

I share my story with this experience being one where I went down the rabbit hole, made it back alive, just to go down it insanely again because I feel a lot of people would've drawn a huge red line in the sand there. I can honestly say, that I know, if it weren't for the grace of GOD, I would not be here. He is the only explanation I have for surviving the miraculous near-death events that happened in my life, and I have only come to understand all this in recovery.

A recovering brother, House, once told me, "The difference between GOD's grace and GOD's mercy is that GOD's grace is giving us a beautiful life we don't deserve. Whereas GOD's mercy is keeping us from the ugly life that we do deserve." Lord knows I should've been dead many times over. I should be somewhere in a ditch with a double-tap entry wound in the back of my head, faced forward, pushing up daisies. But here I am. I live an amazing life that some people can only dream of, and I owe that all to the creator. Another thing I learned from recovery is that praying is me talking to God, meditating is me listening. My brother Jeshua used to say, the easiest way to meditate is to breathe in with GOD, out with Manny, which is still a struggle for me.

Oh, and everyone in the SHU that was participating in the fight that day? Hooting and hollering and rooting and kicking? Well, the guards rightly figured how it played out. After the shock therapy that was administered to me, they scrapped the plan and decided it wasn't so bad to go without yard and food for a couple days or so.

There's a story that reminds me of the islands that I think I should share because I think it is relevant to the story I just told you. It's about a young boy and an old wise man.

The old wise man and the boy were on a canoe going downstream when the wise man looked up at the sun and skies and said, "Son, in your lifetime, have you ever studied astronomy or astrology? You know that our people used only the stars to circumnavigate the globe through voyaging, and used the stars for counting the days?"

The young boy looks up and says, "No. I can't say I have," embarrassed that he hadn't.

The wise man said, "Son, you're wasting your life." The canoe continues downstream.

The old wise man looks out into the wilderness at all the flora and fauna, the plants and animals, and turns to the young boy and asks, "Son, in your lifetime have you ever studied biology, zoology, or microbiology, how living organisms make up protoplasm, and how protoplasms make up living matter, and how this makes up life?"

The boy again looked embarrassed, put down his head and replied, "No wise man I can't say I have."

The wise man repeats, "Son, you're wasting your life." The canoe continues downstream.

The wise man puts his hand in the waters and attempts to catch a small fish then turns to the young boy and asks another question. "Son, in your lifetime have you ever studied biological oceanography? Or marine biology? The way plants and fishes survive underwater whereas they can't survive in fresh air?"

The young boy repeats again, "No wise man I can't say I have,"

The wise man repeats, "Son you're wasting your life".

Only this time, the boy looks up ahead and sees a 50-foot drop coming upon them at the end of the stream and turns to the wise man and says, "Old wise man, I don't mean to interrupt your studies, but there's a 50-foot drop at the end of the stream. In your lifetime, have you ever learned to swim?"

The wise man says in a panic, "No, Son, I can't say I have."

The boy then replies, "Well, you can know everything and anything there is to know about the world, but if it doesn't save your life, you wasted it."

    I tell this story because it's analogous to my life and how sometimes I can be so intelligently blind and oblivious to the most obvious things. I know many who are too smart for their own good and have tried to figure it out for themselves, refusing help. Many of whom went down a much deeper, darker, longer, and narrower path to recovery. One of the first things I noticed when I came to recovery was that I would always tend to overthink a lot of things because of my intellectual nature and I suffered for it. I always future tripped, worrying about the future, and because of this I suffered in the present. Not knowing how to focus on the here and now. Not sticking to the present affected my reality. An old timer named Jim once said to me, "If you sit there quietly but observingly long enough to grow mold on your butt, you might actually get sober." He taught me what it meant to always stay in the NOW. He would say, "You could be sitting here while your mind and heart is somewhere else. Which at any rate, you're wasting both of our time."

    I only understood later what he meant. It was hard to meditate and stay focused if I was always looking for a mental escape. A distraction. A break from reality. Even when someone was talking to me, I'd zone out to another planet. Jim would say, "Mission Control to Apollo 14, do you still read me?" Haha. Rest Easy Jim. I'm still listening and learning because of you. I'm still present. Thank you for my sobriety.

CHAPTER FIVE

Unfortunately, you would think this experience of being shocked would alter my behavior path and mindset, changing the trajectory and course of my life, right? Nope. Real alcoholics like me go through many excruciatingly painful experiences, some near death. When we survive them, it would embolden us to be worse, not better. In Drop the Rock, a book on recovery, it talks about how the pain of staying the same has to become greater than the pain to change before we even consider changing. And even then, many of us come into the rooms just long enough to have the pain subside, and then we're off to the races again. We try things our way with hopes of fulfilling whatever grandiose idea is in our heads with one more great attempt, ending in one more miserable failure.

When I was young, I got whatever I wanted when I wanted it. More accurately, I took whatever I wanted when I wanted. A lot of this behavior, I believe, had to do with being the baby of eleven kids. All my siblings would always coax me to beg my Mom or my Dad for something they would want because I'd most likely get it. If I didn't, I would throw huge tantrums and eventually be subdued with whatever it is I wanted. As I gradually got older, not being given what I felt I was entitled to led to me taking it. I had a friend introduce me to shoplifting and from there I was off to the races. Living like this though, was complete and utter chaos. It led to me growing up doing what I felt without regard for the consequences and the dangers it posed on others and myself. It made me selfish or more selfish, I should say. If I wanted something, there was nothing I wasn't willing to do to get it. If I believed wholeheartedly that I deserved it, which I always did, I would not let up until I possessed it. This is how demanding with tantrums the things that I wanted that were provided to me as a kid, made me adjust poorly into my adolescent phase and adulthood. By twelve years old, I was leading a pack of thieves, robbing, stealing, and burglarizing my neighborhood.

There's this thing that I saw online that said, "In the embryonic stages of life, humans are considered deuterostomes. Meaning we develop as an anus before anything else. Unfortunately, some of us never develop past this stage." It's funny because, for a long time, this was me. I think my feeling entitled made me super optimistic in my expectations. It made me not accept no for an answer. Shakespeare said, "Expectation is the root of all heartache." And boy did I know heartache because of this mentality. I hated being disappointed. I know I needed to change a long time ago because this wasn't my only error in thinking, but by the time it became obviously painful, it was too late. I felt I didn't know how. My thought process was so distorted by twelve that I lived that insanity as my normal. I had so many thinking errors ingrained in me from childhood that I became a walking character defect. I had passed the chance to change on a train to destruction a million miles ago, and the only thing I could do was to keep riding to the bitter end to see it through. I was like that kid that moms would yell out, "Car, car, car," and bang, I'd get hit anyway.

In the SHU, I had ample time and opportunity to look over the riot incident and all the crazy events that took place in my life. I had the time to occupy my mind with more healthier coping mechanisms by getting into the programs that they offered. Instead, before I could fully reflect on an incident, another one showed up and I was forced to deal with it instead of processing what just happened. The riot, which I was in the SHU for, started because the warden neglected getting involved when I told him to. Seriously. I had been targeted at this particular prison because of my previous leadership role in the places I had been. When I showed up, the warden came to see me. He asked if I was going to be a problem. I said, "Nope. As long as your staff don't bother me, I won't bother them." I was active in prison politicking and pushing the line (enforcing the prison code of conduct) everywhere I went. When I arrived there, I was nearing home and was trying to stay out of trouble. The story of my life though. Trouble follows me like a loyal dog. Boohoo for me.

I shouldn't have expected people to sympathize with me because I wanted change when it was convenient. I built that reputation and had to live with it. I don't blame the guards. The thing that blew the whole situation out of proportion was the SWAT team, the highway patrol, county officers, along with the media showing up. We were on every news outlet in the state and made national news. When the media was filming us taking over the prison, I guess waving at the cameras and yelling, "Hi Mom. there's not going to be any visiting this week just letting you know," didn't help either. Nah, you're right. Throwing the fire extinguisher through the window blew everything out of proportion, but you know.

Something that typically happens with inmates who've been in the SHU for long periods of time is we develop these nightmares. I remember one day, in solitary confinement, waking up screaming "HELP!! HELP!! HELP!!" I found myself trapped in a blue suede decorated coffin. I was struggling to move and break free when claustrophobia started settling in rather quickly. I was helpless in my attempts at breaking this coffin door open, and all the fears and anxiety that came with the realization that when I got out of this coffin, there would be six feet of dirt I would need to climb, gave me a panic attack. My every attempt to break free was futile. I tried and tried to no avail. I finally gave in to the realization that I was probably going to die buried alive.

But if that were the case, I would at least die trying and giving it my best efforts, so I started slamming my head against the coffin door with all the strength I could muster up, in whatever limited movement capacity I was allowed. When I slammed my head against the coffin door hard enough, I woke up with the biggest headache ever. I was having a recurring nightmare and didn't know it. The reason I felt like I had woken up in a coffin was because I had slid myself under the bunk bed in isolation, which is a really tight space close to the floor. I guess the feeling of a constricted movement made me dream that I was inside the blue coffin box. The only reason I slept under my bed was because I was completely naked and had no blanket or sheet to cover myself with, and the cold was eating away at my bones. I realized I was under the bed when I saw the graffiti that someone had smeared under it. It was a guy professing his love for Jenn with a heart around her name drawn in blood.

When I got up from under the bed, I felt this overwhelming and comforting warmness. It was one of the most calming feelings I have ever felt in my life, and when I looked up from rubbing my head, I could swear I was not alone in the one-man cell. I was in there with something that was smiling down on me. I jumped and ran to the door and started kicking with every ounce of strength I could gather up until I had broken my toe. In isolation, you are not given a blanket or sheet to avoid inmates utilizing them for suicidal purposes. I screamed and hollered and yelled until my voice was gone, and everyone started screaming back because I was causing such a disturbance like the weirdos who kick the door all day and scream their heads off. But the guards never came. I guess they must've been short staffed again.

When the nurse saw me the following week, my toe was the size of a golf ball and all she could do to help was offer me ibuprofen and tell me to drink lots of sink water. It was a cruel joke because you don't get water in isolation to avoid inmates flooding their cells. This is why isolation cells are called "dry-cells." They leave the sink water turned off. I had pills I couldn't take. The typical doctor recommendations in prison for pain are ibuprofen and exercise by walking laps.

A lot of inmates I've spoken to that have been down here a while say that they experience these too. The dreams of dying. The dreams of being murdered. I think having anxiety makes me prone to having these recurring nightmares. But the feeling I had in that SHU after the nightmare was different. Today, I know what that feeling and experience was that made me bust my toe in that cell. The only way to explain it is that it's a spiritual experience. I feel the same feeling of comforting hope and peace enveloping me tightly and comfortingly when I'm praying. This warm and soothing sensation says that everything will be alright. And it usually does turn out that way. I can only explain this experience as spiritual from learning about it through researching spiritual books.

I believe the recurring nightmares came from anxiety build up that really was triggered by fear. The fear, which I believe subconsciously, came from my parents' continuous threats of me not going to Heaven if I continued on my troublesome path. I lived my life not caring about dying but afraid of going to Hell. The opposite of many who I thought wanted to go to Heaven but didn't want to die. I was never a religious kid because in church, as a little boy, I had the false idea that God was this angry and jealous God, and that he was insatiable. There was no way I was going to please him. I think, because of this, I pretty much wrote God off at an early age and adopted the mentality that I was an orphan in the universe. I was just like a lot of people who aren't even living. Just merely existing. Whenever I felt this feeling that I now embrace, I avoided it, which is crazy. To think that I was afraid of genuine peace. The feeling of calm. I was uncomfortable without drama. I was told many times that I was addicted to it.

There's this story from the movie Sleepers that perfectly describes how I lived. I'm like a guy who falls asleep drunk at the wheel after binge drinking the night away, and my car careens over a cliff. I wake up just in time to jump out and then find myself hanging on the edge of a steep precipice by a tree branch, yelling, "HELP!! HELP!! HELP!! IS ANYBODY THERE?" and then the Heavens part open, a bright and blinding light illuminates and breaks through the skies accompanied by a thunderous voice, which starts talking to me saying, "My Son, Let go. It is me. I will save you." And I immediately turn away from the light and yell, "HELP!!HELP!!HELP!! IS THERE ANYBODY ELSE?"

You see, every bad incident and situation I've been

in, I always felt like something was trying to morally compel me to stop. Something was telling me to put the shovel down and stop digging myself into a deeper hole. But like I said, I just didn't know how. This is something I've heard many others say coming into recovery, which really is an excuse. If I really wanted to change, I could've shown some willingness and seek out that help I needed, or accept the help that was offered to me. I could've put the shovel down and called for a rope. But like Drop the Rock tells us, "We change when the need for change is greater than being the same." The problem is, we don't want help or have trouble asking for it. We often say we didn't know how to as an excuse to relieve ourselves of the responsibility to do so. I believe that we are all meant to be evolving creatures. God never changes, but we do. If you think about it, dinosaurs, animals, birds, and every other creature that didn't have the ability to adapt, acclimate, and change all became extinct. It's the evolutionary process that keeps us surviving.

For some reason though, change is the hardest thing to do. I have met men in prisons who would rather be stuck in an 8 by 6-foot cell, than trapped in a 9 to 5 dead-end job in the community. All because of the fear of change or the excuse that they don't know how to. And I get it. We're comfortable avoiding having to deal with the fear of change by not dealing with it at all. We avoid it so much that we remain the same until it's extremely unbearable or extremely uncomfortable and fearful, that it gets harder to do so. Fear fosters resistance, and resistance is a byproduct of reluctance. But the minute I started doing things differently, and making it a routine every day, discomfort dissipated. That discomfort is replaced with feelings of strength. For me I allowed that feeling to become nurturing and comfortable until the uncomfortable became comfortable. There are men in prison that have had all the eagerness and desire to change.

They get out and come right back in. Is it because they didn't want to change and were faking the entire time when they were here last? No. I am sure they really wanted to. Either they were unprepared for things that occur with change, or they were short sighted on their plans and didn't follow through. Some returned to the same influential environment where the temptation was overwhelmingly great, thinking they could overcome the temptations that came with it. I was always hopeful for someone else's change because I didn't believe in mine. I know me. In the back of my head there was this echo saying, "You'll never change. Don't even think about it."

When I would ask guys that came back what happened to bring them back, it was the same thing. Drugs, alcohol, or women. Not necessarily in that order. Frighteningly, for me, the guys I was hopeful for usually came back. They were the ones that everyone thought for sure would make it out in the free world. I hate that they do come back because it sometimes solidifies other inmate's beliefs and convictions that change is unreachable or even worse, impossible. I'd always remind my friends inside, that the ones who we knew had a spiritual personality before they were released, and followed through in growing and refining that personality, are the ones that we need to look up to. These are the ones that have made the impossible possible. Sadly, most of them who do make it in the free world don't have time to reach back and tell us the secret to their success.

CHAPTER SIX

"Hi, my name is Manny and I'm an alcoholic."

Like I said, I had the J.G. Wentworth syndrome: it's mine and I want it now. I was going to do whatever I wanted, get whatever I wanted, and no one could tell me otherwise. Growing up and building a bad reputation because of this M.O., I became what people wanted me to be. My teachers in elementary school would say, "You're going to end up in prison someday." To which I would respond, "I'd rather be in prison than have to see your ugly face every day." I was fixed and determined to be the worst of them with a booster and energy pack included. I'd say it was all part of the growing pains and count it as just another experience. I had savagery hammered into the core of my existence. I had savage blood running thick inside my veins. If you told me someday that I'd find GOD and that I'd be running around talking about his mercy and grace, I'd have probably given you a savage beating thinking you were insulting me.

A lot of the influence on my bad behavior came from growing up the grandson of a violent chief in Samoa. Hearing about his brutality and strength, made me idolize my Grandpa like many of his grandchildren did. My Grandpa was feared. Respected. Loved. I think a lot of me wanted that power. Even at a young age, I felt that yearning to be revered like royalty and loved with loyalty.

The version of Grandpa's story that was told to me when I visited, was that my Grandpa was an alcoholic through and through and he was violent when he drank. The dirty secret I didn't know and discovered was that my Grandpa was half white. He was believed to be the son of a German soldier. Back in those days, in the 1920's, Germany monopolized the cocoa processing market that Samoa was rich with. It is believed that my Grandpa's dad was part of the patrolling forces that kept Germany's stronghold and reign on the market imposed. Because my Grandpa was white, he grew up fighting for his place amongst others in our family circle. He fought because he was mocked. He fought because he was disliked.

Back then being a half breed was a sign of disgrace and betrayal to the culture so I could imagine why he became a violent brute. To make a short story shorter, he died young. And when he died there was a huge celebration throughout the neighboring villages as well as his own. My Grandma said the streets were flooded with mobs screaming sounds of joy and hope now that Grandpa was gone. It was like a small country that celebrates liberation when an evil dictator who ruled it dies. To ensure the people there wasn't a sequel to Grandpa's reign of terror in the council, or his violent legacy carried on, his oldest son, my uncle, who was said to be his heir and successor, was killed shortly after. My uncle was about 14.

At ten years old I started drinking and got arrested

for the first time. By twelve, I was living with a 17-year old named Nelly Estes (name changed for privacy reasons, but IYKYK) and I was doing grown folks things, which I had no business doing. I was an alcoholic through and through by the time I was thirteen but was in great denial of it. I would do any other drug available, if only I took my first drink. By this time in my life, at thirteen years old, my best friend, "Gargamel" and I, were responsible for almost all of the car thefts and burglaries in and around the neighborhood and known around the state by other car thieves and burglars. Like I said, I was already leading the band of thieves to a career in crime.

My drinking got so bad that it eventually landed me in the Castle Medical Center Psych Ward in Kailua, Hawaii, upstairs on the second floor where they kept the adults. I'd been drinking that day and spouting off suicidal and homicidal slurs. I rushed the police when they arrived for a disturbance call, and don't quite remember what happened exactly, but I know I got pepper sprayed and taken to Castle Hospital. I had my stomach pumped, while ironically being fed charcoal. Their diagnosis: Alcohol Poisoning.

At the age of fourteen, I was sentenced to juvenile life, which meant being sent to the Hawaii Youth Correctional Facility until I was 20. In 1993, I was part of a heinous crime that would change the waiver age for children to be sentenced as adults in the state of Hawaii. Since I was just a juvenile, I couldn't be sentenced to more than my juvenile life for a murder charge that rocked the State. The judge, feeling I had gotten away with murder, with him wanting to sentence me alongside my brothers to open life sentences but not being able to, immediately pushed for lawmakers to introduce a bill that would change the waiving age. That way, when a minor commits a violent crime, he could be sent to an adult prison for 20 plus years, instead of just until he was 20 years old in some youth facility.

Before I tell you about the crime that landed me in the youth corrections for all my juvenile life, let me tell you about Castle Psych ward because this place was a real trip. It was one that flew over the cuckoo's and eagle's nest for sure.

I woke up in 5-point restraints in the psych ward, tied down to the bed after being arrested and fed charcoal. They let me out into the unit later and I was able to play with all the other fun time characters there. I had the bitter taste of charcoal still deep in my throat and was resentful of the medical staff and police. I remember not wanting to be friendly but meeting a guy who, I would say, is the friendliest person I've ever known on this earth. A guy I'm going to call 'Stitches' because he had about 30 stitches clear across his neck from one side to the other. Supposedly, Stitches tried to sever his own throat and failed.

Stitches was Filipino-Hawaiian, heavy set older man about late 40's at that time. He was quite a prankster. He could always be seen with a mischievous, garbage eating grin on his face looking like he was up to no good. He introduced himself to me by talking bad about the other patients, and we hit it off.

I'm going to tell you more about Stitches later but let me introduce the entire crew first so you can visualize the crap show that went on in that place. First, we had this girl that would freak out and start yelling, "DON'T LOOK AT ME. DON'T LOOK AT ME. HE'S LOOKING AT ME, HE'S LOOKING AT ME," when no one was looking at her. She was a tall curly hair thick Asian, islander looking woman. This woman would start shaking violently when she threw her tantrums, and it would trigger guys in white suits that looked like NFL pro-football players to come rushing into the wing and tackling her into the floor until she was pacified by a shot of thorazine in the butt. I walked by her not even knowing that my mere presence was what set her off; that's how much I was looking at her.

She would often talk to herself and say to an invisible audience, "This is my husband," pointing to an invisible spot next to her. She would go on, "I had a wedding ring but I had to pawn it." She'd hold up her empty ring finger like that was proof enough that she pawned her ring. And as crazy as she was, I don't know if I was any saner because every time she told that story about her husband in an ear shot of me, I'd always break my neck turning around to look, curious as if her real husband would show up somehow when she introduced him. Except her real husband had died when he broke the fall during his and her, Romeo and Juilet suicide attempts off a balcony. I think I had the FOMO (Fear Of Missing Out) syndrome with not wanting to miss seeing who the lucky fella was because she got me every time with that. That was my real diagnosis if you ask me.

Next, there was a guy that ran around saying, "I am Jesus. I am HE. Bow down to me." He would stand on the chairs so often and do his sermon on the mountain speech, that it would trigger the NFL white coats to come in and take him down for disturbing the peace. This guy didn't know when to quit. As soon as they'd let him back out to play with the rest of the cool kids, he'd act up again and start preaching in rants and get the white suits again.

Lastly, the most memorable of them all. A golden glove boxer who had suffered from one too many blows to the head that he would become suicidal from it. He was suffering from what I believe a lot of ex-NFL players do. Chronic Traumatic Encephalopathy (CTE), a progressive brain condition that's thought to be caused by repeated blows to the head and repeated episodes of concussion. It's particularly associated with contact sports, such as boxing or American football. But back in the early 90's it wasn't known enough to be called what it is today.

Another person I can't forget was this beautiful smoking hot Asian Hawaiian looking Nurse. Every time the white coats would come in, this beautiful, big chested, honey brown-eyed girl of a nurse named Bridgett, with two tees as spelt on her name tag, would come waltzing in behind them with a huge needle the size of a magnum highlighter pen, full of thorazine, and stick it to us in the butt. I attempted to flirt with her during the pill line one day, and all I had was, "What a job. Sticking people in the butt." Not one of my greatest moments, I'll tell you. I was so in love with her that I would've allowed her to stick me with 50 giant needles. Ok, maybe not. But if you're reading this I still love you Nurse Bridgett. Haha.

The boxer was the most memorable of all these other characters because he had a hair trigger personality and was always looking for a fight. He was dark, short, and mean. He had a left hook to match it too. He was athletic and built, and had a miniature afro that looked like a huge black boxing glove on his head. He was always exercising and training inside his room. Stitches would often mess with the boxer by pulling one of Stitches' ole mischievous pranks. Anytime someone would pass the boxers room, they'd have to be careful not to stare at him or say anything because he was easily provoked to fight without you knowing exactly what you did or said to set that into motion. Like I said, hair trigger personality. Ready to go at the drop of a dime. I would always look down when passing his house because he was like the *menehune* legend on the island, in our unit. A mythical creature that scared people but a retarded version.

One day, I found Stitches taking a spoon and tapping it against the glass so it would sound exactly like a boxing ring bell. Ding, ding, ding, ding, ding, ding!!! The boxer would come out charging from his room ready to fight. And if there was someone outside his door they'd be attacked without warning. I've seen an unfortunate victim heedlessly fall into the traps of this wild jungle occupied by this mentally challenged animal. I saw this sleek golden glove cheetah run down an unsuspecting guest and gun him down at the sound of the bell. It was not a good look. Hearing the sound of bells was the trauma response that triggered the boxer to lose his marbles.

    The boxer went absolutely crazy every time he heard ringing sounds. And every time the boxer would come to the door looking for a victim, Stitches would throw the spoon into his glass of water and conceal it. He'd then stare at the ceiling pretending he was in his own make-believe world. When the boxer would retreat into to his room, Stitches would smile that infamous mischievous smile, and repeat the process. Soon, I joined in on this ridiculousness because I was bored out of my mind. I would conceal the spoon and laugh it up with Stitches when the boxer would go back inside, do it all over again and laugh it up. All was fun and games until one day.

CHAPTER SEVEN

    This particular day, I was walking absentmindedly past the boxer's door. I was spaced out in another world, not even thinking of where I was at or what in the world I was doing here when "Ding, ding, ding, ding, ding, ding!!!" This motherless goat, Stitches! He hit the spoon-glass bell on me and the boxer came out charging like a bull, swinging and clawing. I took a couple shots to the face before I realized the serious dangers of what was happening. I threw a Hail Mary hoping to thwart off further attacks, but everything that landed wasn't enough to stop the onslaught of blows. I was astonished by how I was even standing up after taking all those shots to the head. But I was even more astonished at how this boxer hadn't lost his mojo considering he was supposed to be crazy.

    I finally latched on to him for dear life, while gasping for breath hoping the white coats and my Bridgett would come running in like usual. Always hurriedly for everything else, no matter how trivial. As luck would have it, they must've been having lunch or something on this day because they took their sweet ol' time. It felt like an eternity. By the time they showed up I was so gassed and winded from trying to hold this boxer that I didn't even resist. I just fell to the ground exhausted and threw my hands behind my head with my butt up in complete surrender. The beautiful nurse stuck the needle in our butts and it was fade to black. I just want to say, Stitches, if you are reading this and I hope you are, I hope your Italian necktie healed up into a beautiful scar, and I forgive you, but you are still a motherless goat for that.

After that incident, having been shot up with thorazine, they restrained me to the bed for the day. When the doctor let us back to our rooms later, my dad came to visit and prayed over me. I remember watching my Dad crying his eyes and heart out, begging and pleading with God to deliver me. The only spiritual thing that I remember happening was the guy proclaiming to be Jesus came into my room to use my bathroom and flushed the toilet numerous times in a row to where the noise of flushing drowned out my Dad's prayers. I could not sympathize with my Dad even if I had wanted to. I was so far gone, removed from the spirit that all I could do was sit there and watch my Dad cry and beg.

I'm writing this because sometimes we easily normalize things in our lives that wouldn't be, but because we refuse to see it for what it really is or was, it becomes normal. This is something I learned from Jim. That the rabbit hole of my addiction is mental. He said alcoholism was a slippery slope for me because I refused to live in the real world. I never understood that until I had more than two years of clean and serene time. I was only 14 when I made my visit to the nut house and at the time, I couldn't understand the disease and addiction of alcohol. To me it was just another experience of growing pains in becoming who I thought I needed to be, and the psyche ward was a perfect jumping point for a crazy life.

My Dad's story is kind of strange in how he found God. My Dad used to be a full time drunk. I remembered my dad drinking all the time when I was younger. He always had a beer can in his hand. I remember when I was three-years old, my Dad shoved my mom out of our moving car where she was sitting right next to me. It was very frightening to me to see my mom go flying out the car in the middle of the road at three years old. I also remember an incident where my Mom had crab boiling in a pot for my Dad's supper which he poured on her. He had burned her so bad she had scars from her shoulder down to her wrist. I remember my Dad having this look of genuine apathy like the woman he was beating was someone he didn't know or love. My Mom tried to leave my Dad but he wouldn't have it. He always begged and promised things would change when he sobered up, but everything went back to rage when he was drunk and mad.

My Mom, for whatever reason though, was so strong in church that she would attend faithfully every Sunday. My Dad wasn't much of a church goer then and I liked that because I didn't like going to church. I hated having to pretend to be a well-behaved child when in truth, I wasn't. I could always cry to my Dad when my Mom would try to force me to attend services and my Dad would tell my Mom to leave me be. It was great. On occasion when my Mom did lure me to church with the promise we'd go get ice cream after, it was like anything I did caused my Mom to hush me or swat me. Hence my great dislike for attending church service. It seemed like me moving around during church was forbidden. I remember people crying and shaking and talking about Hell. I did not want any part of this. It was creepy to me. As a kid, I couldn't understand any of it and I just wanted to do me.

One day my Mom lured my Dad to church and the only thing could be said for that was a miracle. Not that he made it to church, but that it affected him so much he was never the same. During the altar call that day – where they called people up to the front, my Dad went up and fell on his face and cried like a baby. Following that Sunday, he stopped drinking and started looking forward to church services. He attended Bible Studies. Bible School. Prayer Meetings. Weekday church services and stayed glued to his Bible. He was so consumed by church activity that you'd have to go to church just to talk to him. At home he was so involved in reading the Bible that he would not come out of the room.

My Dad later got his pastoral degree in Bible college and became a pastor. He started his own church and got all his kids involved in the church band. My Dad went on to help build the First Tongan Assembly of God church in the United States and traveled throughout the west coast putting roots down for this congregation in different states. He did in the 90's what people are only doing now. He was on radio doing podcasts and became a big radio personality because of it. By the time my Dad stepped down as a pastor because of the COVID-19 epidemic, my dad had 33 years of service to the church. He is over 33 years sober. I say his story is strange because, to me, I couldn't fathom or comprehend the magnitude of what occurred in church that day to make him fall on his face and change. I fell on my face millions of times, and for the life of me, I only woke up with black eyes and broken noses. Strange.

I want to make clear that prison and the psych wards have nothing to do with making a man of me. Recovery did that. Prison and the psych ward, neither are my story. Finding and trusting in God is. My mental health recovery is also the result of this same faith and belief that I found in my recovery from alcohol.

When I was incarcerated in the youth corrections, they had me diagnosed with so many mental health illnesses that would later be dispelled with time and truth. The Youth Corrections facility I was incarcerated at would later undergo a federal investigation. It uncovered so much abuse from sexual, physical, and later, mental health as well. I first experienced pills through this place. I remember being zombie-like and just zoned out on meds. I was like the walking dead. I remember having nine different doctors and being prescribed twelve different psychotropics like paxil, depakote, trilafon, mellaril, trazodone, fluoxetine and many other medications in a matter of four years. Some of these medications have been discontinued because of long-term effects. You could ask the doctors for anything at the place and they were more than willing to crash-test-dummy you with it.

I had a doctor who was probably studying to get his Ph.D. or MD in need of field practice. He prescribed me some things that drove me bonkers. After a short while that doctor left and the next soon to be doctor would show up and prescribe me something else. They'd test for the results and the side effects, get their reports, and leave. They guinea pigged us and didn't care about the lasting effects this had on us youth inmates. They cared more about testing to see if my limbs were locking up as part of the side effects from pills than if I got better. It would all seem legit considering that the state was getting free mental health care from understudies from the local universities. Sadly, most of the kids that I knew from that place on pills ended up in really worse places and doing crazy things. Some ending in high speed chases and shootout with cops and others in shooting sprees. I think there is a strong correlation between medication and violence, which is ignored and needs to be better looked at. The correlation is blatantly too obvious to be disregarded but yet it is. Big Pharma will probably hate me for this but what do I know? I'm crazy.

The reason it's so imperative for me to make known that prison and psyche wards is not my story is because I know guys that spent a few months in jail give talks and go off on a rant about prison like it's something to be proud of. A lot of testimony preaching nowadays is just a form of entertainment. It's more about being comical and entertaining, drawing likes, rather than telling it like it is and letting the truth of it all be the deciding factor for interest. In my life of crime, I'd always tell guys that I'd rather be hit in the face by a friend than kissed on the cheek by my enemy. I hated being lied to. I was always paranoid. I always needed to know the truth no matter how bad it was. My lawyer (sponsor) telling me like it is, and not sugar-coating things, is what got me sober. If he came in with a song and dance, telling me lies, I'd have probably thought he was full of it and carried on with finding ways to get myself killed.

I've been to prisons such as (Walla Walla or Wally World) Washington State Penitentiary, Clallam Bay, Federal Corrections and other sordid places, spending over 20 years of my life inside of a cage. Having done so, I want to make it clear. It doesn't mean that I'm tougher than you, it just means that I saw more men naked at one time than all of you did in a lifetime. That's all. There is nothing tough about prison because it's the easiest life without any thinking involved. You don't have to worry about bills and taking care of your responsibilities. Everything is provided for you. You get three hots and a cot. No thinking involved.

I ask guys that speak of their prison experiences in recovery if they have ever tried that as a pickup line? "Hey baby, I just came home from prison. Do you want to come to my mom's house and make bologna sandwiches?" They get stuck. They have this perplexed look on their face like I've asked if it's morning or night time when the sun's clearly out. The only hard part about prison is adapting to the politics. The realest tough guys I met were guys that got out and are managing their lives on the streets taking care of business. Guys that are going to work and taking crap from their bosses and not losing it. Going home and taking crap from their wives and not lashing out. Dealing with their children's hard days and still remaining sober to show up at their kid's games and recitals. Guys that are legit and motivated by real life's challenges to take it one day at a time. That's the real challenge. CHANGE.

CHAPTER EIGHT

Ironically, I said that while I started writing this book sitting on a metal bunk bed after having been sentenced to a 10-year mandatory prison sentence in a Federal Correctional Institution for distributing large quantities of methamphetamines to states across the country and to the Pacific Islands. I regrettably helped pollute and contaminate the south pacific islands with drugs. I must say that in no way do I glorify any of what I did, nor do I condone my past life of crime and active addictions. I'm embarrassingly writing this in hopes that I can circumvent a kid, who is like me, from going through these things I unnecessarily went through because my ideals were screwy. I am writing this in hopes that the awareness would bring others to find a better alternative solution to their challenges and struggles in the streets. In no way is this book to educate anyone on the ways of improving their criminal lifestyle or negative behaviors. Furthermore, this book is not to aid or assist any law enforcement albeit state, federal, or local in understanding the machinations of a gangster or criminal mindset. This book is solely meant to be educational only, and the purpose of sharing my whereabouts and experiences relevant to explaining how, in a world of chaos, I came to finally find CHANGE.

America's deep fascination with the gangster lifestyle and the romanticism of it all is almost inherently the allure for most children born in poverty and raised in the housing projects I was raised in. Every kid I knew growing up idolized the grown-ups on the corners hustling and making fast money, hand over fist. I was one of those kids that saw that as an inspiration for a future career and not a hustle. The thing they don't tell you about this lifestyle is that there's nothing romantic about being stabbed in jail or being shot in the butt at a bar. Or how the gangster lifestyle betrayed me and everyone that stays solid in it. You are always having to watch your back not just from your enemies, but also from your friends as well. You are always being hated on and targeted by someone.

In Mario Puzo's, The Godfather, he says, "Keep your friends close but keep your enemies closer." What he never tells you, which is apparent from the movie, is that your friends today may be your enemies tomorrow. And that is the lifestyle in a nutshell. Against my better judgment I'm going to tell this story of how deeply the poison of betrayal runs in the drug cartel life. They say blood is thicker than water. Well, this story will show you how much thicker money ink is to them than blood.

My "connect" had a cousin that was bringing in shipments through my connect's secret routes. Upset that his cousin was doing this, my connection tried hopelessly to get him to stop. They were trying to back door his every deal and sabotage his every shipment. But the more they tried, the more the cousin saw areas in his routes that needed improvement and started getting smarter and tighter about his deliveries. He was being made aware of where his shipments were falling short by all the failed attempts at disrupting his supply, that he actually tightened up and became good at it.

Meanwhile, my connection was losing money and clientele because they were seeing that the cousin had better prices, and were jumping ship. Scandalous as the cousin was, he even approached me with a more lucrative offer and a huge promise which was his biggest mistake. One thing about me is that loyalty is everything. That saying, "Blood makes us relatives but loyalty makes us family," goes a long way. So, one day my "connect" asked me to hijack his cousin's biggest shipment to date. I agreed with the exception that I keep most of it for myself and my people. I had to do the recon work and provide the muscle, which I had the best resources for, so of course I expect the lion's share of it. I had ex-military personnel and ex-cons that worked for my security business at the time so this was a cinch. After pulling off the job I gave my "connect" his portion of the spoils. Meanwhile, the cousin went back to his suppliers in his country and tried to explain that he got robbed and he needed more supply to recover his loss. He promised he would triple their return in their investment if they resupplied him, considering and basing this on the fact that he had the most tight and secure method of delivery.

What he didn't expect was that the suppliers had already struck a deal with my "connect" and were raising the prices per shipment and no longer needed the cousin's services. And to make sure he didn't disrupt their steady supply, and sabotage their new brokered deal, they made him disappear. Not long after, the cousin's brother came to my "connect" asking for help. He couldn't return home in fear that he would befall the same fate as his brother. I mean, somebody had to pay for the lost goods. He didn't have any means of making money and didn't know the routes and trade secrets, which vanished with his brother. I watched my "connect" turn around and give the cousin's brother the portion of the spoils I had given him and asked him to work that off using his brother's former clientele.

Years later when everyone was growing prosperous off the Polynesian triangle pipeline, my "connect" himself disappeared. I learned that the spoils he gave his cousin's brother were given to the suppliers to prove that my "connection" was behind the shipment getting hijacked in the first place. They used my "connect" until they no longer needed him, then he was good as gone. If that betrayal doesn't get you, then the large indictments handed down will because it oozes into the sewer streams of which gangsters swim. Many of which turn and mutate but not into fighting turtles, mostly Master Splinters. The Rat. I'm going to leave that right there for the young aspiring up and upcoming gangster in the streets that is probably addicted to more things than one and doesn't know how to get out of his situation without fear of losing respect from his peers, or fear of overcoming that mountain. I know youngsters that are trapped in fear of leaving because they think it's like moving a mountain.

I tell of the gang upbringing because I grew up in it, with all the virtues and codes they live by. I am no longer surprised when old heads break codes and cooperate. I will say that my distorted beliefs were what made me fear change. It warped my ability to sympathize, empathize, or love. It has kept me closed minded and standoffish to anything that could help me change. It blocked my path to spiritual enlightenment and kept me worldly ignorant and blind. Engaging in this attitude and distorted belief is what held me captive by the fear of leaving and kept me imprisoned and hostage to gang life. It's politics.

CHAPTER NINE

Everything has politics in it. Prisons have politics. Gangs have politics. Police have politics. The government has politics. Wars have politics. Corporate offices have politics. Churches have politics. Even church bands have politics. It's what kept me imprisoned in my own dark corner of the world having only a skewed view to look out from. Always finding the differences and not seeing my similarities in others. It caused me to be cold and callous to anyone and everyone not from my inner circle. You hear it or read about it every day when people say or post on social media, "Keep your circle small." Well, my circle was so small it was the size of a period at the end of a sentence. Yes, it's politicking.

It caused me to be biased in my opinions and thoughts. It's caused me to feel comfortable with a division between me and you as long as you and your views stayed on your side of the world. But this ideology is cancerous in that it's killing communities across the nation. It is the cause of civil unrest and social injustices. If we focus on our differences instead of our alikeness, we will never adapt to the greater purpose of God's will for us – to peacefully co-exist. To live and love your neighbors. To be aware and have your REAL-eyes, REALize, the REAL-lies.

In 2017's Presidential Election, when President Trump was elected into office, how many people got sucked into savage government politicking and drew their own dividing lines between them and the world they didn't want to know? How many church goers allowed government politics to ruin their church connections with others? How many people started to cut off longtime friends, family, or other loved ones because of political affiliations? I've watched supporters for one side of the aisle call the other's leading candidate the "antichrist," while the other side called them "devil worshipers." Sadly, recovery went through the vortex of insanity over politicking too. It was like more and more institutions, churches, and rooms that's supposed to be a safe haven and refuge for people like us became more secular rather than spiritual. Like instead of the message coming out from these sacred places into the world, the world's message was filling the chairs and pews. And sadly, it left a lot of people in a state of heightened social anxiety and fear.

In 2008, I made a business friend with a guy that started a technology company. This guy created what is known today as the RFID reader. The price gun that Flo from progressive auto insurance carries. The price gun that is now so common that Walmart stock workers carry them and simply point at a bar code and can read the price and every detail about the product. The technology was initially created for canoe racing. They would put the sticker on the front end of the canoe and when it would reach a buoy that was used as a finish line marker, the buoy that would have the laser tech mounted to it would scan the sticker from the canoe to tell the exact time the canoe crossed the finish line. The technology was also for marathons and long running races, where the sticker was on the person's number. The finish line would have the technology mounted on the post and can read the racers finishing time. This technology is worth millions and millions of dollars, and I got to be part of it.

My friend had a multimillion-dollar deal with a Rental Car company where we would put the sticker on your bag when you checked in. When you arrived at the airport the information boards would scan your sticker and send a message to the rental car company. The rental car company would then send a bus to pick you up and have all your paperwork ready to where all you had to do was sign and drive away.

Unfortunately, during this time the country went through one of the worst economic crises ever with President Bush handing over $700 billion dollars to Wall Street and the biggest bankers in the U.S. to deal with. This federally funded program, known as Troubled Asset Relief Program (TARP) did nothing for the country besides keeping the rich richer. I don't think people realized the gravity of 2008's financial situation and how catastrophic that financial crisis was globally. It impacted financial institutions all over the world and it all started with the fall of the Lehman Brothers subprime mortgage company. AIG would have been the next in line had the bailout money not come from the government. When Obama took office, following the start of this recession, he bailed out the automotive companies and airlines without any consideration of the smaller businesses that helped make those industries thrive.

How I got involved in this business deal was that there was a rum company in Nicaragua that was once owned by the Nicaraguan Presidential family. The guerrilla army, or rebels as they are better known, had taken it over. They exiled the presidential family to the state of Florida in the United States (real story can't make this up) and started operating as rum runners. The rebels had taken over 500 acres of the sugar cane fields that are used to produce this rum and ran this rum company for themselves. The problem with it was they had an excessive stock pile of liquor and didn't know how to manage their inventory. The barrels that were out there sitting the longest, had a potency value that would make the rum value increase. Instead of halting production and figuring their storage situation first they just kept pumping out barrel after barrel of liquor. Trouble was they were confused which barrels were which. As a result, the rebels reached out to have my business friend fly in and micromanage or fix their inventory problem. Using the RFID reader, he could simply put stickers on the barrels and then point the reader to it and it would give full details of when it was produced and every detail about it.

The fear was that since these were rebels or outlaws, for lack of a better term, there was a healthy degree of fear that came with doing business with them. One of those fears was that they would probably end up holding my friend hostage and having him work for free or something worse. No offense to rebels or mercenaries out there. I know this seems stereotypical of us to judge your business, but this type of thing happens all the time on TV. So, sorry. Where I come into the picture is that I can speak Spanish and ran a well-known security business at the time. My job would be to escort him into the country heavily armed with a security detail that would protect the deal from going south, no pun intended.

Up to this point, I ran security that extended throughout the city of Tacoma and up towards Seattle, Washington. We employed a lot of former military staff and ex-cons but to think that we would hold up against rebel forces was a bit of a stretch. So, I got involved and struck a deal with the rebel's company myself. The rebels loved me. They love someone who operates like they do. Someone who believed in a cause. Someone who looked to long term expansion and not just temporary profit. The thing that they were lacking in, besides inventory smarts, was sales and distribution know-how. They were also locked into a distribution deal that was holding them financially hostage because they were seen as nothing more than rebels. How stereotypical of the distribution company. Shame on you.

The rebels, try as they may, were not taken seriously as global market players. They were seen as thugs with a business and the distribution deal that they had prior to taking over made it almost impossible for them to move cargo globally. I suggested that I take the excess inventory in the form of containers from them. Since I had control of one of the most active pipelines of drugs coming into the country from Mexico, why not? It was simply a win-win. BUT. And I know, once someone says but, everything before that doesn't mean anything. BUT, yes, I wanted to take everything they sent me and relabel and redistribute it under my own brand. Under my own company. Run it my own way. I know that I could've done more for them then they could have on their own and was taking more risk with having to bypass customs, border patrol, and every other delivery issue. Trucking it from Mexico is no easy feat. So, I took that deal over and made it work.

We were going to launch a liquor company called Millennium and introduce my new brand of rum under new catchy names. Instead of a Kahlua Mudslide we would introduce the Milky Way. Instead of a Smith and Wesson, we had an Excalibur. Instead of a Long Island Iced Tea we had a Jupiter Drive. I tell this story simply to tell you, yes, I snatched this deal from a friend because even business has politics. I thought I could do better. I was wrong.

Savage politics is ideals, values, and beliefs that ignore, denotes or discriminates against any other person's identity, race, sex, or creed. In this case I undermined my friend's intelligence because it was in my nature to think I could do better. My beliefs were that I had a more dominant creative outlook and superior intellect on business than he did. Being judgmental of my friend caused me to be a bad business associate. I no longer care what you do or believe. I will not judge you. Differences have always been the division between us. If we look, we will see we are more similar than we are different.

One of my favorite quotes by Obama, "I reject a politics that is based solely on racial identity, gender identity, sexual orientation, or victimhood generally. I think much of what ails the inner city involves a breakdown in culture that will not be cured by money alone, and that our values and spiritual life matters least as much as our GDP."

SAVAGE BEAUTY

1 Peter 3:3-4
Your beauty should not come from outward adornments, such as braided hair and the wearing of gold jewelry and fine clothes. Instead, it should be that of your inner self, the unfading beauty of a gentle and quiet spirit, which is of great worth in God's sight.

CHAPTER TEN

I have met many men inside prisons that honestly say, "This isn't my last rodeo. I'll be back." I'd think to myself, "Wow, there's a real cowboy for you. I'm hanging up my colts because I'm done." Yet these guys haven't had enough. They lick their wounds and get right back to crime and alcohol/drug use when they get released like it ain't no thing. It's like prison is a detox vacation and nothing more. My old cell mate talked about being caught like it was an accident that wasn't his fault. I think these guys are crazy. But that's a drug dealer's life for you. I'm not going to lie, when you are around this kind of prison gibberish all the time, it's like a mental assault. It makes you wonder and question what you know. What if these guys are accepting that this is just their nature and there's no changing this? What if I'm fooling myself into thinking that I could be any different when I'm not? What if I'm doomed to a life of crime and punishment? What if this? What if that?

I experienced this feeling of insecurity when I first sobered up. I started feeling out of place. Like I was fooling myself. Like I was faking it. This thinking is dangerous if you don't have a filter or strong awareness of it.

If you're reading this and you're spinning your wheels from self-loathing and self-doubt, it's normal. Especially if you have a bad track record to re-enforce and validate your doubt and fears, it's even more intensifying and real. But I've met people in the free world who have this same issue of self-loathing and self-doubt and it's not just a prison thing. For me, the strength and will to beat the odds wasn't in me. The perseverance to thrive and live legitimately wasn't in me. I had the same attitude of it wasn't my fault, or this ain't my last rodeo, when I came into prison the first few times. Accepting defeat before you start makes failure so much easier. I think it's more challenging for someone who knows they got what it takes to make it, and still have this low self-esteem and skepticism because they know better.

It wasn't until I was sure of who I was and what I wanted to be that I could see beyond the mountain of fears in my view. This mountain was what blocked me from living a life beyond my wildest imagination. I just had to take this giant leap of faith to get over it. I just needed a willingness to remove it. Not having the faith and willingness to move this mountain made me come up with excuses like, "This view ain't so bad." I convinced myself with excuses so much that I felt like unless I was in a burning building with a small window of opportunity to leap from, I wouldn't. I was skeptical of being released and questionable of success in the real world at first because prison is conducive to self-loathing and self-doubt. I think questioning your worth is normal until you make it an obsession. Then it becomes a real issue.

Fearing the unknown has this apprehension about

it that gives me anxiety and panic attacks like I've never known before. There's a unique stress associated with getting out of prison that you will never know unless you were getting out. It's almost this crippling restless, irritable, and anxiety feeling that will make you not even want to get out of bed. A lot of men stay up all night because the anxiety and mixed emotions is too much to sleep through. Wondering what's the first thing you're going to eat when you get released? What's the first thing you're going to do? Who's the first person you need to see?

Writing helped me find myself in a sense that I was able to identify the true feelings of what I felt and know that they were just emotions. Nothing more. Just because I felt like the sky was falling, doesn't mean the world was ending. Or just because it felt like everything was good didn't mean that life would now be easy peasy chocolate squeezy. Life is a pendulum of stresses that come and go. Knowing that I had the power to overcome the hardships and check my emotions alleviated the unmanageability in my head. Reading also helped me a lot, which is what led to me wanting to write a book that I believe could be useful to someone feeling the same effects of stress.

"This too shall pass," is a saying my brother in recovery, Jesh, used to say to me a lot. When visiting me in prison he'd always remind me. This Persian adage which was written into a poem in 1867 by American newspaper editor and abolitionist Theodore Tilton, is a timeless piece. It's so powerful and profound that I wanted to share it. It's something he'd send me that hung up on my wall to remind me to keep things in perspective.

<u>The King's Ring</u>
Once in Persia reigned a King,
Who upon his signet-ring

SAVAGE RECOVERY

*Graved a maxim true and wise,
Which, if held before his eyes,
Gave him counsel, at a glance,
Fit for every change or chance;
Solemn words, and these are they:
"Even this shall pass away."*

*Trains of camels through the sand
Brought him gems from Samarcand;
Fleets of galleys through the seas
Brought him pearls to rival these.
But he counted little gain
Treasures of the mine or main.
"What is wealth?" the King would say;
"Even this shall pass away."*

*In the revels of his court,
At the zenith of the sport,
When the palms of all his guests
Burned with clapping at his jests,
He, amid his figs and wine,
Cried, "O loving friends of mine!
Pleasures come, but do not stay:
Even this shall pass away."*

*Lady fairest ever seen
Was the bride he crowned the queen.
Pillowed on his marriage-bed,
Whispering to his soul, he said,
"Though no bridegroom never pressed
Dearer bosom to his breast,
Mortal flesh must come to clay:
Even this shall pass away."*

Fighting on a furious field,
Once a javelin pierced his shield.
Soldiers with a loud lament
Bore him bleeding to his tent.
Groaning from his tortured side,
"Pain is hard to bear," he cried,
"But with patience day by day,
Even this shall pass away."

Towering in the public square
Twenty cubits in the air,
Rose his statue carved in stone.
Then the King, disguised, unknown,
Gazing at his sculptured name,
Asked himself, "And what is fame?
Fame is but a slow decay:
Even this shall pass away."

Struck with palsy, sere and old,
Waiting at the Gates of Gold,
Spake he with his dying breath,
"Life is done, but what is Death?"
Then, in answer to the King,
Fell a sunbeam on his ring,
Showing by a heavenly ray -
"Even this shall pass away."

When I first introduced the idea that I was writing a book to friends and family, it seemed everyone had thoughts for it. It was suggested that I should focus on telling about the drug trafficking exploits and expeditions involving my Mexican cartel connection and conviction. Some thought that I should write more about my life of crime and make the central focus of my book about business endeavors that

I ventured into while doing so. Others thought I should just write about both the Polynesian triangle and the Mexican golden triangle's connection bonded in a supply and demand relationship.

I decided to write a book on recovery because I do not identify with those other things any longer. I do add stories that explain why I struggled with change. Why the struggle to go legit was a big part of getting sober. But for the record, I'm a completely different person today than I was ten years ago. If you knew me then, and met me now, I'd have to reintroduce myself to you because that's not who I am. All my trials and challenges that I got through and passed over me like a distant cloud, none was as tough as changing and getting sober. Recovery and God are, by far, the hardest things I've done in my life. If I haven't lost you yet with my jumping from one subject to another without a smooth transition, trust me, this too shall pass. There is a method to the madness and somewhere in between the lines, someone will get sober. I promise.

Although I have to admit, when I first started writing the book, all the strategies and implementations in the applications of power and legal exploits that I used in gaining experience in 'the life' (gangster's life), did come easy to list. One of the business endeavors I dove into was herbal medicines. Not particularly marijuana which might be people's first thought. Although I did have an interest in CBD oils before it was popular but no, not that kind of medicine.

We had this company that produced nutraceuticals instead of pharmaceuticals. Products that were all-natural, plant based as opposed to chemical. One such product it produced had better results for glucosamine control and dealing with diabetes than anything on the open market. The company also had a pill with milk thistle as a key ingredient, which increased liver function and cell recovery that was popular with patients that had cancer and going through chemotherapy. A lot of the products produced by this company didn't just prevent diabetes and cancer, they had real testimony proving it.

The company, founded by a doctor who got his MD-PhD at the Harvard Medical School of Medicine and Research, would have been successful today. The doctor, finding that natural medicines produced better results in recovery than pharmaceuticals, quit working for the Big Pharma industry and he and his wife started their own company doing all-natural healing in Washington state. The thing that attracted me to the company was that culturally we believed in healing from the land. The other reason, of course, is that it was outlawed. The (FDA) Food and Drug Administration had little interest in companies that provided millions of testimonials results instead of clinical trials. The other reason I believe that the company was facing all the opposition and legal hurdles it did, was because it opposed Big Pharma companies.

This company wasn't just doing research on natural remedies and medicines. It was researching other companies on the market that promised "100% natural" ingredients in their face washes and skin lotions, when in fact it had Dimethicone, polyethylene, and other harmful synthetic ingredients in it. Ingredients that may pose a dangerous side effect to consumers such as skin irritations, rash, hair loss, and eczema. The odd thing about it is the U.S. FDA only bans around eleven chemicals out of the thousands out there used in skin care, shampoos, body washes, and other hygiene products. Yet since they had no interest in natural medicine studies, our company was outlawed. They did allow you to use it and give it to friends and family. But they didn't want it sold on the open market. Sad. Last I heard about the company, the owner and his wife moved out of the country to where they could help and profit from healing people. For a long time, I wondered how many lives would have been saved had that company thrived in America.

As mentioned, I did use strategies and implementations and legal exploits in my life. I wonder how my life would have turned out had I not used gray strategies and implementations in my life. Insights and tricks I learned from reading a library of political philosophy, war time psychology, sociology, and whatever else-ology books, which made me an educated dummy but personable and a valuable asset to my past associates. I read books such as my favorite, Machiavelli's "The Prince" (which I kept a copy of when I was running the streets) and I vowed that if I wrote a book it would be titled, "The King," because I felt I had reached heights of wealth, political power, and street cred that made me like an underground royalty in my city of Tacoma. I had reached heights that kids from my city could only wish to rise to.

In retrospect, having 100 men at your command, willing to do whatever you think is necessary, legal or illegal, to further a cause is not easily achievable. Going from making hundred dollar deals in parking lots, to making hundred thousand dollar deals in company boardrooms is not easily done. Buying a commodity for $3 thousand U.S. Dollars from Mexico and reselling it to the island's drug markets for $80 - $120 thousand dollars is what a broker/dealer in the stock market can only dream of.

And yes, like everyone that comes into this kind of fortune, from illicit drug sales and criminal rackets, I did party like the Wolf of Wall Street. I had women looking like Playboy Bunnies, and spent recklessly like a Billion Dollar Whale. I mean, I blew a boatload of money on every vice known to man. But what does it matter? It was all ego and in my recovery program, they tell you that ego is not your *amigo*. It doesn't matter what you had, only what you have left. So, at the risk of not wanting to sound like a prison guy telling war stories of the past life they lived, yet coming home to nothing because it was all lost during the raid or while they were away, it's irrelevant.

All these ideas that flooded to my mind, when I first started writing, didn't align with my current faith and beliefs. The good thing, however, was that now I had a list of things I didn't want to write about and could better focus on things that I did want to. My bother Jesh would tell me all the time, "This too shall pass. Meditate on the message before you write." And I finally get it. People ask me all the time if I'd do it all over again. If I had another chance at "the life," would I do it all over again? I'd like to be honest with you. It took what it took to get me to where I'm at in life. Sometimes it takes something really bad happening in order for us to realize we need change. That something bad happening could sometimes be a near death experience or even getting incarcerated. For me, prison wasn't bad enough. Getting shot wasn't bad enough. Getting shocked wasn't bad enough. I finally just got sick and tired of being sick and tired. It took everything bad enough to be bad enough for me.

CHAPTER ELEVEN

In my life of finding myself and understanding the beauty within me, I discovered that I had to be true to myself. Alcoholics Anonymous awards colored chips for remaining sober. They look like poker chips and each color corresponds with an amount of time in sobriety or if a person is renewing their sobriety. There is a Shakespeare quote printed on the chip, "To thine own self be true." I want to tell a story that I think is relevant to trying to please people and explain why I took a different approach to writing the book on recovery.

The story is about the same boy and old wise man in the previous story. But this time they go to the marketplace to buy a donkey to help them in their field work. Shortly after arriving after miles of walking, they buy the donkey and decide to both ride the donkey back home. As they passed the first village on their way home, the village people razzed, "Look at these idiots, they just bought this poor donkey and they're trying to break its back before it's even seen in their field." So, the boy got down and the old man rode the donkey alone.

They passed the next village, and the people scoffed, "Look at that poor boy, that old man has stronger legs and should be familiar with long travel. That boy's legs will be useless by the time they get home." So, the old man got off the donkey and let the boy ride.

As they passed the next village, the village people complained, "Look at that young boy. He is so disrespectful letting his elder walk while he sits on the comfort of his donkey resting his young legs. He ought to be ashamed of himself." So, they both walked, guiding the donkey.

As they passed the next village, it was the same thing. The villagers belittled the old man and the boy for walking alongside a donkey that was perfectly capable of being rode back home. Stopping to think what to do next, they both came up with an idea for the old wise man to carry the donkey.

As they crossed the river on a loose manmade wooden bridge, the donkey kicked and fell into the water. The old wise man looked at the boy and said, "Son, if you ever should come into the possession of a donkey, never please another man, should you let them decide for you, what to do with it."

The point I'm trying to make is, it doesn't matter what you do, you will never please everyone. The world is full of people with unrealistic expectations and high standards that you can't reach. If you bought a donkey, who cares what you do with it because it's yours. Knowing who you are and what your purpose or calling in life is, makes circumnavigating the world easier with understanding that you can't compromise your character for the satisfaction of others.

This power of discernment comes easily when you

start doing what's best for your spirituality in recovery, and not do for others what they think is best for you. You will see how fast people change around you when what you do doesn't serve them. How you react to their change by distancing yourself, isn't a poor reflection on your character I should add.

One of the things I had to learn in recovery was that I needed to look at things from a fourth dimensional perspective. The person who says, "No," in a relationship is in power and being that alcohol was my true love, I had to look at things in terms of relationships. Being in that toxic relationship for so long caused me to be blinded by bitter romance. It's the love/hate and volatility of it all that broke me. It was like a breakup when I stopped loving it. I had to change the people, places, and things I knew. It's like breaking up or divorcing your wife of years. Your old friends are friends of hers and you don't want to go around them because of the awkwardness. You don't go to the places that remind you of her. You change things that revive her in your mind.

One of the hardest things about that, for me, was letting people go. I don't really have a lot of people in my life because I am hard to love. So, the few people I do have, I've kept even though they weren't healthy for me. One of the challenges of finding myself and loving myself was because of this. When you long for people to be in your life desperately, you do anything to keep them. In recovery, I found that I had to leave to love women properly, and not like property. This doesn't come easy though when you don't know what love is. Finding a filtration system to keep good people in your life can be a double-edged sword sometimes. I had to identify people in my life that didn't want me to succeed but have been in my life all along.

The late rapper Earl Simmons (DMX) had a powerful quote that I keep in mind, which is, "Always trust everyone to be themselves. But trust in the fact you can see them well. It takes too much energy not to trust someone; you always have to stay two steps ahead of them. Trust people to be them. Trust a snake to bite you. Trust a liar to lie to you. Trust a thief to steal from you. Trust them to be them. But know them when you see them." Sometimes we can't see the real person because we've listened long enough to be distracted by their lies.

Rod Stewart's lyrics in his song, Reason to Believe, states it perfectly.

> *If I listened long enough to you,*
> *I'd find a way to believe that it's all true.*
> *Knowing that you lied*
> *Straight-faced while I cried,*
> *Still I look to find a reason to believe*
> *Someone like you*
> *Makes it hard to live without*
> *Somebody else*
> *Someone like you*
> *Makes it easy to give*
> *Never think about myself.*

I've endured a lot of hardships in trying to find my true self in sobriety. Transitioning into a new lifestyle can be confusing, as well as challenging. It took finding the right people that supported me in my trials to make the changes work for me. It took time and space from people who were the hardest to say no to.

Some people might not consider what I've done in my life as a success, but I say, if you set your mind to becoming the thing you want to be the most in life, and you become it (especially at a young age) how then are you not a success? Whether that be a good success or bad success. It's a success.

I don't speak of the things I've done in my past or gone through in my life to glorify anything other than my God that brought me through it. This book is about freedom in sobriety. How I've found true lasting freedom in recovery. The steps I took to enjoy the joy of living almost normally. The spiritual gift of love that recovery offers. Consequently, it's blended into a mix of chaos leading to change so it may seem erratic. I say this because being clean and sober in recovery is not just about abstinence from drinking and drugging. Recovery in the sense that I'm speaking of in this book is living without it being a constant urge, thought, or craving that makes walking through life like walking through a field of landmines.

The transformation of lifestyle and ideas made it hard to stay sober, at first. I was used to making money the way I always did. I was used to the people I've had in my life as I always did. Getting sober and adopting spiritual principles made me go broke and I was alone. The struggles became apparent with time, but I wouldn't know had I not gone through it. When I sobered up I was, in a sense, like my Dad finding God. Except, I didn't have the spousal support like my Dad did. I didn't want to bother with nothing but recovery.

At about six months in sobriety, I started getting complacent and feeling lost. I started avoiding meetings. The self-doubt and fear started creeping back up again. Feeling the feeling of "I didn't belong," ate at me. Trying to find a job and employment with a lengthy rap sheet was tough. I didn't know how to live sober.

"You only know what you know," an old timer used to tell me. How true is that? Beyond the range and reach of my knowledge, I didn't know much. I'd be guessing, speculating, conjecturing. Most of the things that I knew at that time of my life with six months sober didn't come as easy life lessons in the form of an "aha" moment accompanied with having someone to talk to and discuss it with. Everyone I knew partied. Everything I knew was hustling. I had a sponsor, but you can't expect them to live your life for you.

An old timer named Deric used to say, "I didn't come to recovery to quit drinking. I came to learn how to start living." It took years of praying, reading of spiritual books from the Big Book, Bible, Quran, Torah, Book of Mormon, Buddhist materials and the sweat lodges to understand what I do now. I was in hot pursuit of spirituality when I sobered up again because I wanted what everyone in recovery seemed to have that I felt I didn't. I only knew what I knew, which was going to meetings and fellowshipping. Sadly, that wasn't enough to keep me sober. I relapsed after a year of sobriety.

I was in hot pursuit of spirituality when I sobered up again because I wanted what everyone in recovery seemed to have that I felt I didn't the first time. I say the transformation of lifestyles was hard because even though I was changing on the inside, I still looked like the same person on the outside. I still talked the way I always did, felt the same as before. I ended up in prison again, and in prison, I came to the realization that my talk, my walk, my demeanor was my identity. My voice was my identity. How I spoke and carried myself was that of a gangster.

I remember one of those lessons coming in a hard form of realization. I had met men who were part of the large prison population having been arrested for distribution of drugs. Hearing them talking about their case and the little success they had in the drug trade was annoying. I'd hear them exaggerate their story in portraying earnings as huge wins, when I knew better. I'd be annoyed by their story and how they just one day decided to become drug dealers because of the lure of making fast easy money. When in truth it was their addiction and greed, coupled with the idea of making fast easy money, that led them here.

I met lawyers, councilmen, police chiefs, and every kind in between who were incarcerated for drug trafficking. That baffled me. I'd talk to them and think they'd know better. Like, somehow, I was different. I would sometimes mock them, that they woke up one day without no training or experience and tried to outsmart and outwit the Federal Drug Enforcement Agency, whose officers have gone through 200 hours of classroom instruction, 150 hours of firearms training, 150 hours of tactical instruction, 110 hours of legal instruction and 300 hours of practical applications. Work 100 hours with K-9 dogs, receive leads and daily updates and help from the other 1,000 agencies in the law enforcement network, daily briefing and meetings, assistance from confidential informants, quarterly mandatory refresher courses, and the list goes on. How did they think they would succeed when they should've known better that the game was designed to fail? How could they not have known from their previous careers that this line of work inevitably ends in death or prison? Why did they think getting involved with drug dealing was okay? It's no wonder they were doing a ton of time for a small quantity of drugs.

One day while arrogantly mocking some guy, an old timer that attended meetings with me said something that knocked the wind out of my sail. He said, "Well what makes you so special? You're sitting here with everyone else, smart guy."

I was taken aback because, really, with all the things I did to circumvent capture, and not being on that side of the law before, I felt like I earned my place in this large population of drug trafficking failures. At one time, I had people all over the states in different regions bombard the post offices on the same day with hundreds of gifts for kids in the islands. All the boxes were smeared, with residue and dust from dope without containing any actual dope inside. I figured I would outsmart the dogs because if the dogs sniffed on all the boxes that had to go through Hawaii to reach the other Pacific Islands, it would be overwhelmed.

When they'd inspected the packages to find it didn't contain anything but actual candies and gifts, they'd be confused by the number of empty packages the dog would hit on. Eventually they would think the dog was crazy and retire the dog. Then all the other packages containing the actual dope would go through easy peasy. The only thing that ended up happening was we slowed the mail down to a screeching halt to where the shipments were late on arrival.

The Postal Inspector, Brett Willard; D.E.A agent, Nick Jensen; Homeland Security Agent, Joseph Abrew; U.S. Customs Agents, and the F.B.I agents, who were part of the combined Federal Task Force that took me down, noticed that there was a common theme in the boxes being that it all contained candies and gifts inside. They seized a total of $351 thousand dollars heading to me in Washington state from Guam, and pieced together the idea that it was payment for the packages that they didn't catch because of their dog sniffing problem.

I had been studying K-9 dogs and discovered that they possess up to 300 million olfactory receptors in their noses, compared to about six million in ours. The part of a dog's brain that is devoted to analyzing smells is about 40 times greater than humans. I found that if you took dope and put it in a peanut butter jar, then put that jar in a canister of oil, then took that and put it in grease, and then put all that into a in a plastic tube that was dropped into a truck containing gasoline, that the dog would be able to smell the drugs, the peanut butter, the oil, the grease, the plastic tube, all the way to the gasoline that it was dropped in. We had corrupt, federal agents working with us, which gave me the false security that we were going to be protected and everything would work out. And still things went awry. When I was later indicted, I found in my paperwork that it was a dog named "Rico," an official agent of the law (paperwork enclosed for viewing in the Appendix) that sniffed out all the packages and eventually brought my seven-year run to an end. I know some people might not consider what I've done in my life as a success, but I say, if you set your mind to becoming the thing you want to be the most in life, and you become it (especially at a young age), how then are you not a success? Whether that be a good success or bad success, it's success.

I wanted to tell the old timer that people don't think or care about learning things like I did. They just think, "Well, it can't be that hard. I'm just going to purchase it in bulk, and it'll fly off my kitchen shelves into the streets because this thing sells itself." I wanted to tell this old timer that people don't realize it's not easy coming up with ingenious plans that the feds ain't heard of, to smuggle things over the southern borders and across to the Pacific, considering that 46% of the federal inmates are behind bars for drugs, and most of them are in there for being first time drug entrepreneurs.

I used to sit for hours on end and create a plan of attack to send packages because I wasn't in it for the lifestyle, I was in it for real. People that are in it for the lifestyle are just people in the way. They're actually not in the game like I thought I was. I was in it for survival. They were in it for the gold chain and status. Hence, my "connect's" cousin who became expendable. It's these people that don't know what they are doing that get others caught up by trying methods they don't know the inner workings of. They end up getting the routes and methods caught and exposing these new routes and methods to law enforcement who were unaware of it before. My "connect's" cousin did get good at it but that's the fear of people already doing things. That someone does these things without thinking and jeopardizes everyone, which is how I thought of the guys I mocked.

As I was going through these thoughts in my mind it shamefully dawned on me. At that very moment it hit me like a ton of bricks, again no pun intended. But anyways, I came to that important realization. I didn't know anything about recovery. Everything that I knew had been in a year of being sober. Which, at that time was just going to meetings and consorting and bonding with people in recovery. Doing the steps but not living it. Sponsoring people but not helping them. What did I know about sobriety and developing a new identity? I knew more about being bad than I did good.

All the bad things I knew made my life a chaotic atomic nuclear wheel of energy, with everything I touched turning to destruction and despair, was my identity. This far overshadowed the things I knew about recovery and being a decent human being. My identity was that of a major drug dealer which is what I wanted to become in life. But it wasn't who I really was because most drug dealers end up dead or don't see capture as a failure, just a minor setback. I was more focused on recovery and how I would get back sober before I got incarcerated. I was more worried about how I'd come out instead of going in. I didn't have a clue about real sobriety and although I could impressively recite the "How It Works" entirely from memory, that knowledge without experience was miles and miles long short of wisdom. In short, it was going to take doing the difficult, the uncomfortable, and the almost impossible for me to change and prevent a future relapse.

"You can't think your way into a new living. You have to live your way into a new thinking," a mentor in recovery used to tell me. I didn't realize that up to that point, my identity was who I thought I was and not who I needed to be in order to exact the change I desperately needed. I also came to see that who I thought I was and who I wanted to be, would often collide in daily struggles. I might have had the outward spirituality, but the inward personality remained the same. The truth never tasted so much nastier than it did that day. Like eating rotten oysters that were sitting out in the sun for days (don't ask me how I know). The truth be told, the most embarrassingly funny but not so funny thing, was I didn't get busted because of the dog. No. What brought everything down was cookies. Them dang Oreo Cookies. Yes. Oreo cookies took me down.

CHAPTER TWELVE

So, you're wondering how Oreo cookies took me down right? Haha. Well, it happened like this. My little sister who lives down a few houses from me begged me to come over and cook these marshmallow treats at my house. Me being a fat boy at heart, thought, "Oooh yeah. I want some. Come right on over."

She comes to the house and cooks these Marijuana edible Fruity Pebbles marshmallow treats. She leaves them on the table and leaves. Meanwhile, I'm running errands and when I get back to my place, it reeks. I could smell this smell from outside the driveway. But naively, I didn't think anything of it. I come in and see these marshmallow treats and think, "Ooooh yeah. I want some." So, I eat one of them and go back for another. I like them so much that I'm going back for a third piece and a fourth and I couldn't stop myself even if I wanted to. They were that dang good.

I soon found myself famished and starving for cookies. I had packs of Peanut butter Oreos, Mint Oreos, and Party Flavored Oreos and took them all out. I sat at the kitchen table with a glass of milk and when I opened the peanut butter Oreos I noticed that the first cookie was turned inside out. For some strange reason this freaked me out. Being involved with drug sales already gives you a heightened state of paranoia. But on this day, I was extremely paranoid yet didn't know why. I called my Mexican family in Texas and started talking about Oreos. This is the conversation that pretty much gave the feds who've been tapping our phones exactly what they needed to convict me.

It went like this:

> Mexican Family: Hola primo. I wasn't expecting you to call until next week.
> Me: *Compa, alguien está jugando con mis galletas* (someone's sabotaging my cookies).
> MF: Why you say that?
> Me: I just opened the brown pack and found that the first cookie was turned inside out.
> MF: Oh yeah? Well, we don't sell brown cookies. Only the crystal and the white ones. Where did you get it from?
> Me: WinCo's. They have sales on them and I always buy cookies in bulk.
> MF: Wait, you're working with another Cartel? WinCo's? Where are they from? As far as I know that territory is pretty much all ours.
> Me: Nah bro, WinCo's is nationwide. They sell everything cheap. I bought the brown ones, the green ones, and the party flavored ones from them.
> MF: Party flavored? Is that a new kind? I've never tried that before. I'd probably like it too much

anyways. Hey, I'm going to call down south and find out about this new group operating in our spot. Meanwhile, don't buy anything else from them. If you want to knock them off line I can send guys to help you guys."

Me: Nah, my little sister can handle it. I'm going to send her back there with it and file a complaint.

Following that conversation, I called Guam. The conversation went the same. The only person who was spared from these calls was my cousin from Hawaii. He was so dumb that ignorance is a bliss sometimes worked for him in this scenario. He answered back saying, "See, *thas* why I no buy those kine Oreos. I only like the orange ones. Halloween flavored! Yeah. the sad *ting* is they only come out with those during Halloween. I wonder why that is?"

Following my relapse after that first year getting sober, I got back into operating. I went back into the life harder than before. I got sober again, but it was almost a year after relapsing that life finally whooped me. It took me an honest hardworking nine months to get one week of sobriety. Yes, you read that right. It took me nine months to get one week of sobriety. And just as I was doing everything right in the world, everything that could go wrong went wrong. I was six months sober when I got indicted and was looking at 20 years in prison for things I did during my year-long relapse. My mom, who was my greatest love and support, had died. I had a newborn baby who I would not see for 20 years, possibly. I was being harassed by the Feds that I was putting a hit list together. The list seemed endless.

I was 35 years old, six months sober for the second time, depressed and questioning everything about faith and recovery again. It took me a year to get sober after relapsing because I believed recovery didn't work. I was going to meetings and trying to get sober but I was finding myself leaving the meeting and going to the gas station to get gas and get drunk. The old timer Deric, who talked about coming to recovery to learn to live, would say, "The worst place to be stuck at in recovery is having a belly full of alcohol while having a head full of recovery." He knew that it worked for me the first time around and watched me grow in my recovery. He knew that I wanted so desperately to get sober but was struggling.

People that don't know think, "Well why don't you just stop?" Which is an oxymoron for an alcoholic like me because I could never understand how normal people could have one drink then just stop. Deric and a guy named Ted used to put on this sobriety workshop called, Do the Steps or Die. Ted would break down alcoholism and genetics for me one day. He said, "Alcohol is like diarrhea. It runs in your jeans." Meaning, if you have a genetic predisposition to crave alcohol when you drank, you were screwed. Deric could see that I was questioning myself when I was saying things like, "I'm looking at 20 years in prison while Purdue Pharma lied about opioids being addictive which killed good innocent people, paying off large fines in settlements, and they get off scot-free?" Seeing how 80% of the opioid users started with prescription pills and every day at least 90 of them die from overdoses.

Deric taught me about accepting responsibility and accountability for my part in everything and not blaming others or things for how my life was turning out. It was probably what I didn't want to hear at that time, but it's what I needed to build my character. Build my identity.

My lawyer was saying things like, "Maybe God wants you to take the message where not so many people can go." At six months sober I had the toxic thought of trying to rationalize, minimize, justify, and blame everything I was going through on other people and things. I was still at a toxic stage, emotionally, where I couldn't understand how I was feeling. I became very depressed and gloomy, and like before, I stopped taking anyone's calls. I wanted to go and get drunk and numb myself from this intense and severe mental pain, but I couldn't. I wouldn't.

Viktor Frankl, a psychologist who survived the holocaust in a Nazi prison camp categorized depression in different stages in his book, A Man's Search for Meaning. He said, "Depression occurs at three levels - psychological, the mind; physiological, the body (oversleeping, loss of appetite); and the spirit. The depressed man faces tension between who he actually is in relation to what he should be."

I was so depressed I think I hit every level of depression falling on the way down to self-pity. Viktor Frankl also wrote that "Life has meaning under all circumstances, even in the most miserable ones. Our motivation for living is our will to find meaning to life." At that time, I felt like my world had come crashing down and I was in a thunderstorm of confusion and despair. I felt the quick sands of addiction trying to pull me back into the dark criminal oblivion. I had thoughts of suicide dancing constantly in my brain. It felt like I had the weight of these temptations sitting on my shoulder weighing heavy on me, white knuckling it. I didn't want to hear anything else about recovery. But it was during these times that something incredible happened. Something that I believe is a divine intervention in the form of relationships we build in recovery.

I had a sobriety brother who himself was fairly new in recovery, named Jeshua. He would text me knowing I wouldn't answer the phone. He would text things like, "God got you," and "God loves you." He'd show up and talk to me through my front door. Relentlessly. So much so that I had to let him in to avoid complaints from the neighbors. He persistently came over and talked me into getting dressed and getting off the couch. He dragged me to meetings, churches, and his house to eat dinners with his family so I wasn't alone. He prayed for me and encouraged me to pray with him.

Jesh would later visit me and write often while I was in prison. It was something that was new to me but is true to the love they have in recovery, and you will find within its communities. This kid would go on for years in his recovery being known for helping others get sober and stay sober. He had helped hundreds of people by taking them through the steps and mentoring them in the process of recovery. It's because of him bringing me the message of hope, the message of change, and the message of God during my most trying times that I'm eight years sober and alive today. It was because of him bringing the faith he had when I was losing mine, that I'm here today. Jeshua would always say, "Let Go and Let God. He's the driver of the bus. We're just the kids in the back seat, wearing helmets and chin straps, making faces in the window. And as long as he's driving and not me, we'll actually get to our destination."

The thing about Jesh is, he credits me for him being sober. He was outside of a meeting that had been canceled one rainy night. He was drenched in sweat and rain from having walked a half a mile to this meeting. I showed up as well not knowing that the meeting was canceled. I saw him sitting out there in the rain and said, "Hey, I didn't know it would be closed."

Disappointed, he said, "Yeah, me too. I need a meeting badly. I'm struggling."

I asked, "You want to go to another meeting across the other side of the bridge?"

He said, "Yeah, I would like that."

From there our friendship ensued as he became the motivation for me going to more and more meetings. I'd call him up or he'd call me up and we'd routinely and religiously go for the hour-long drive to the other side of the state to my home group in Port Orchard, WA. We got active in step work and ran through it the way the old timers did. We started taking others with us to Deric and Ted's sobriety workshops and it was amazing. The chance of us meeting was all God because normally I was unfriendly and untrusting of others when I sobered up or when I was drinking. I wouldn't have even asked him that night to come with us if it weren't for my girlfriend at the time, Amy, yelling through the window of the car for me to ask him if he wanted to go to one far away. People who love us know when we need one. It's usually when we're being jerks. Amy was not letting me go without one because I was being an unlovable jerk that day to where she said, "You're going to a meeting tonight!" So yeah, I needed one badly too, I guess.

CHAPTER THIRTEEN

I want to cover something that I think is very important in recovery and imperative in sobriety. I think it's crucial to maturity, in general. It's what savage beauty is all about. It's about your true identity in recovery. It's about being comfortable in your own skin. I write this because when we show up in recovery, we're not doing it in Cadillacs with smiles, wearing shiny sharkskin suits that we are used to. We are showing up most likely battered, beaten, broken, bruised, used and tormented by our lifestyles that we are just a shell of a person crawling on our hands and our knees seeking refuge. Some of us slithering and squirming like worms out of breath. And I truly believe that God had to let us be broken down from who we thought we were before we could be built up to who he wants us to be because at that stage of our lives, we can't hear anything anyone says to us.

I have truly recognized how a divine intervention has occurred during my most troubling times in life with how the creator kept sending me messenger after messenger. Jesh is one of those people. It is scary to think, had he not been the person he became, I might not be alive today. He struggled with how he viewed himself in early recovery. We both did. I believe we both needed the love and motivation reciprocated in our recovery bond which helped us grow. It was like our bond gave us the missing confidence we needed to battle our insecurities and fear. Jesh was a man with a heart of gold. A kid that everyone loved. A great husband and father. I'm glad I met him that night and saved him from whatever he was going through because he was always there for me when I needed him afterwards. We save those who may later save us, they say in recovery. This is one of the miracles of recovery that is hardly talked about. But this isn't the entirety of the most incredible thing that happened.

    I stress the importance of identity because as a newcomer (someone who is new to recovery), alcoholics are still in the process of finding themselves that we often feel like we don't belong. An old timer talked about how when he first got sober and started going to meetings, he would often hear everyone talk about getting together at the "meeting after the meetings." He so much wanted to go and would often feel like he wasn't really invited. When he did drive to the pancake house where everyone met after the meeting, and he was about to turn in, he'd start overthinking things. He'd say to himself, "What if there's only four to a table and he shows up the fifth wheel? What if I show up thinking I was invited but the invitation wasn't extended to me?" He mistakenly thought. What if he showed up and no one spoke to him? On and on the squirrels in his head would have him spinning his wheels that he would ultimately say, "You know, alcoholics would much rather be dead than be humiliated and rejected." And nothing could be further from that truth.

    I think that we, as alcoholics, get so used to that

false bravado or false sense of identity and confidence when we drink, that when we sober up, we question everything, overthinking. We often don't feel a part of. We easily get discouraged and don't give ourselves an honest chance. I think, for me, coming into recovery for the first time, not wanting to associate, was my subconscious way of having excuses. I didn't go because I didn't get along with no one there. I didn't go because I can't relate. I didn't go because I don't feel welcomed. Yet people introduced themselves to me. People tried to talk to me but I ran away. This was me my whole life, which makes it easier for me to leave when I don't have attachments.

When we drink, we become more sociable and more outgoing, that when we sober up, it's the one thing we miss. I used to hear an old timer say all the time, "We drink to feel good. Well what is it about us that doesn't feel good that we need to get hammered, nailed, trashed, or (whatever other term to explain being flat faced on the concrete) to feel good?" I think the answer to that lies in the comfort or discomfort of this new identity. I think that is one of the hurdles of recovery. I have known people who become successful businessmen working their job like it's an addiction. Even spirituality and refining who they are have become somewhat of a healthy addiction that I think it all boils down to discovering who you are and making that version of you happy, that we go on to excel at roles God meant for us.

In 2014 this is the incredible thing that happened that me and Jesh got involved with which became our identity. While I was on pre-trial, fighting my case, I became this popular kid for starting (for lack of a better term) a cult-like following that became an internet sensation. I started single handedly making baggies of goodies and food, and distributing it to the homeless people in my area. My girlfriend, Amy, was the one that came up with the idea of helping others. It grew from a single act to many people joining me in helping feed the less fortunate in my city.

One of these acts was caught on camera and posted to the internet, and before you know it the movement started and it eventually headed to being morphed into a 501(c)3 not-for-profit charitable organization with about ten volunteers. The movement was so inspiring and motivational that hundreds more people got involved and actively started spreading the message. The thing that was the driving force behind it wasn't so much the popularity of the movement but the story behind it. I was a sponsor to a kid named Troy, who along with his wife Melanie, became instrumental to building this sensation into an actual movement. The message inspired him and ignited and fueled the fire in the hearts of many who saw him as living proof of what recovery could do. The message was simple. CHANGE is possible. Troy had a connection with the church that donated food to us and so like clockwork, we'd have food ready for us almost every week to distribute. Troy's wife, Mom, and a newcomer named Sarah would package the bags with snacks, water, hygiene products, and we'd hit the streets distributing food and spreading the message with other volunteers.

The empathy from people that used to see us run these streets doing bad, and now see us doing good, drew them in to helping our efforts. Stories of overcoming great struggles and extreme hardship was what banded us volunteers together and attracted people who wanted to aid us in our mission. The people that gravitated toward us were those that were inspired by the underdog story. They supported the movement and championed our efforts to show it can work if you worked it. It was the message and the spirit behind it that cleared the path and paved the way for us to steer our vessel towards easy streaks. Everything came easy, from food support to financial donations. Even Little Caesar's pizza franchises in Tacoma, supported us by donating a couple boxes of pizzas for every 10 boxes we paid for. Although the stories of overcoming disadvantages and leaping hurdles and challenges were great, it was the acts of kindness and doing the do that made the message of change all the more real.

Looking back at it, who'd ever thought that a kid from *Kuhio* housing projects would have started something this great. It went as far up north of Seattle to Everett, down south to Olympia, and as far West as Bremerton. It even set one traveler to take the message with him to Oregon, making friends and helping others along the way.

Before I forget, to all who shared their love and support and gave their time and prayers, I will always embrace your help as a gift of strength through the hardest periods of my life. It is what I used to get over the toughest of struggles in prison. Simply, the world is a safer and better place because I'm in recovery, along with other bad people gone good. It is because of your help and support, that others were able to find God and accept CHANGE. From the bottom of my heart, humbly, I thank you.

CHAPTER FOURTEEN

What people don't know is the backstory of how pay it backwards came about. I was sitting on my couch going through my depression and identity crisis and I felt really conflicted. I was in such turmoil that I was being attacked with suicidal thoughts and ideas. It just crept up on me and followed me around like a dark cloud looming over my head.

I got a call from my lawyer one day and he asked, "What's going on?"

I said, "Nothing. I'm just at the house, losing my mind."

My lawyer explained to me that the most dangerous place for a newcomer was inside his own head. He said, "I want you to get dressed, go to the meeting down the street, and ask, is there anyone that needs help. Just raise your hand and ask if anyone needs help. Okay?!"

To which I was thinking, "Okay, how is that going to help me? I'm over here going insane and you want me to go help other people?"

Nevertheless, I did. One person said they needed help moving. Another person asked if I could mow the lawn of a widow whose husband was part of the group. I said, "Yeah, sure why not." Now here I am, this guy who has never done anything for anyone without compensation. A guy who has been in shootouts and been shot. And I'm going to help people because my lawyer thinks it'll help me stay sober and beat the insanity of doing nothing at home? Seriously?! You can imagine my excitement at the idea of this. Nevertheless, I did it. And it did help me more than I imagined. It helped others and inspired a movement.

When I showed up to this lady's house to mow her lawn, she was so grateful. She said, "Thank you for coming. I didn't think you would. Let me show you where it is."

As she led me around the house, I almost fell out crying when I saw her backyard. It was not a regular lawn. It was a rainforest. It was a jungle. She had grass taller than me. It was so tall it almost reached the roof of her garage. What's worse is I asked if she had a weed whacker, or riding mower, or how about a bulldozer, preferably. To which she answered with sarcasm, "Check the garage." Her late husband kept things there. She had broken weed whackers that were outdated and useless. So, I went to the Home Depot and bought one of those cheap electric ones with the orange extension cords. You know the ones that would always break down so you'd have to stop and rewire the plastic cutting wires and go again 'til it broke down again? Yeah. I was not happy. It took me an entire day just to get through half her acre of burden.

When the weed whacker finally broke again, I had had enough. I sat there and called my lawyer because I was going to give him an ear full and let him have a bad day. I called and complained about how I had been mowing and cutting, and doing all these things that not even other religious groups or good people would do for free. I started telling him how this lady didn't even have the decency to bring me out a cold glass of lemonade or something to drink because I'm soooo special that I needed that. I tooted my own horn and was about in the middle of my self-praises when he cut me off and tore right into me. I'll never forget it.

He said, "You are probably one of the most selfish people I know. You know why these other people in the world don't have to do half the things you need to? Because they didn't do half the bad things you've done while on Earth. You have been blessed to live, Lord knows how many times. You have been given so many chances in life. You have gotten away with so many things a lot of people in prison have not. And yet, you do one good thing and want a gold medal and a public acclamation of presidential proportion for it? You don't want to be bothered because you are so busy doing nothing at home, but you're asked to do one good thing, just one, and are bothered by it? Have you thought of drinking all day?"

I replied, "No. I was too busy trying to fix this dang weed whacker."

To which he said, "Well, fix it!" Then hung up in my face.

You know your real friends when they show up to help you move, paint, or cut your grass. Well, that's what the program taught me how to be. A friend to people. How to be useful. My lawyer's words hit me so hard that I sat there in deep thought after that conversation. Yes, my first thought was that he was beep-beep-beep jerk and can take a flying trip on a rocket filled with cow dung to the moon. But my rational sobered mind was telling me after those angry thoughts that he's right. What's right is right. What's wrong is wrong. And what's fair is fair, my older brother used to tell me.

What my lawyer told me was well deserved. I have been selfish my whole life. I was self-serving. Self-interested. Self-absorbed. And this was the root basis for why I was feeling sorry for myself. My lawyer would say, "Poor me, poor me, pour me a drink." In all fairness to this man who has saved my life by bringing me the message that originally brought me to recovery, he has helped tons of people. He has pulled more guy's out of a bar than a bouncer. I have gone with my lawyer, in his sponsor capacity, to take his other sponsees home from a bar on more than one occasion. He has brought the message to hundreds of clients in his cases, even if the message wasn't well received. He has filed a lawsuit against an internet giant that operated as a child trafficking site and won. He has gone on to champion the movement against child trafficking in America and was praised by John Walsh from America's Most Wanted.

I later went around asking people if they needed help with anything. Jesh and I would be useful instead of useless. We showed up and showed out helping many people. It's what kept us sober. Doing things that made others feel good made us feel good and naturally it's what led to the "Pay It Backwards" movement.

I called it Pay It Backwards because we weren't paying it forward. We had to pay off our debts and right our wrongs to the world first. We have taken from the world more than we can ask to be forgiven. We had to make amends and clean our side of the streets before we could even consider paying it forward. We needed to make sure our own house was in order and that we could do things without recognition or reward, accepting only the good feeling of doing so. This is who me and Jesh became.

One day I picked up Jesh at the Walgreens on 121st and Pacifc Ave. We were already running late so I was kind of irritated. He said, "Hold on, this lady needs help." It was an old lady whose car battery was dead and needed a jump. She didn't have a cell phone or jumper cables, and was locked scared and cold in her car. Jesh had an eye for people that needed help that the old woman really didn't even need to ask. He went to her and asked her if she needed help. To which she frightenedly responded, "Yes," and told him what was wrong. Jesh was like that. I asked the old woman, who was scared and cold in her car, to pop her hood. We jumped-started her car and before we left, I said with pride like we were the sober patrol, "Don't worry ma'am we're sober." Jesh nearly choked laughing.

I can tell you this is something we would not be interested in had we been in the streets. Helping people became me and Jeshua's calling, and we loved it. Being of service. He'd want us to jump out in the middle of the streets to help push a stalled car. He'd volunteer us to take the message to detox centers. He just had a heart of gold, which showed in everything he did. He dated this girl that was in a wheelchair and married her before I went away because he didn't want to wait ten years for me to come home. I was the best man at his wedding. He loved her and nurtured her to where this girl became a beacon in a dark world for a lot of others suffering from similar battles. She started spreading her own message of recovery and strength. She's so amazing.

She went on to get a Bachelors and was working towards a Master's degree from the University of Washington. She went on to win the Ms. Wheelchair beauty pageant. This girl was miraculously alive after being kidnapped and nearly murdered. She and her two-year old son had been held captive in a closet for ransom money by the kidnappers. After days of not retrieving any money from her, the assailants shot her six times and left her for dead in the desert. She crawled the lengths of three football fields, while bleeding out, to wave down a passing car to save her own life. It was always refreshing to see her with my brother Jesh, who she made the happiest man in the world.

Sadly though, my brother Jesh passed away a month before I was scheduled to be released from prison almost nine years later and it was heartbreaking. He and his wife visited me for years while I was incarcerated. I could not believe the news that he lost his battle to addiction. I was devastated. Many people questioned his identity and forgot all the good that he did in his life while in recovery. It's like the one bad thing erases a million good ones. We are alcoholic/addicts in recovery. We are never going to be cured from this disease. We are only capable of managing it with God and recovery throughout time. The Big Book tells us:

> It is easy to let up on the spiritual program of action and rest on our laurels. We are headed for trouble if we do, for alcohol is a subtle foe. We are not cured of alcoholism. What we really have is a daily reprieve contingent on the maintenance of our spiritual condition. Every day is a day when we must carry the vision of God's will into all of our activities.

In the Bible, Proverbs 3:5,6 teaches:

> 5 Trust in the Lord with all your
> heart and lean not on your own understanding;
> 6 In all your ways acknowledge him,
> and he will guide your path.

I know this thing is life and death for me. That if I become complacent and content in recovery, like I had done before, I can be in grave danger. We have to stay vigilant and aggressive in our fight against addiction. We can never become satisfied with how far we come, but rather, need to always stay one step ahead of the battle to move forward. The thing that I learned is that there are so many blind spots in this journey that if I had not experienced them, I wouldn't know what the unforeseen trap holes would have been. "We are not saints," it tells us. "We strive for spiritual progress rather than spiritual perfection." I am a work in progress, some people say. I irritably want to say, "Well heck, how much work do you need?" I have seen people in recovery for so long say this and still act the same as when they were actively using. I have to remind myself that I'm no different, that I'm blessed that I've been given a life sentence in recovery and not in prison, and that my every waking moment spent in freedom is owed to making amends to those I have hurt and making right with God.

    The COVID-19 pandemic caused alcohol consumption to rise and set so many people back. People who were sober 20 plus years relapsed. So, I know that I'm no exception. In the program of recovery, one of the most important things that helped me overcome what held me back was willingness. I wasn't willing to be real with myself at first, and learned it the hard way. I had to allow others to help me. I had to accept encouragement and support. I had to be willing to try something new. All the things that held me back when I should've given myself a chance and changed a long time ago wasn't a lack of willingness alone. It was creating a defensive personality by lashing out instead of reaching out. I drove myself deeper into despair rather than accept people in my life trying to help me to the light. I allowed the lack of confidence in myself, alongside fear, to boost this persona that I was always angry. But even Helen Keller could see through that. The aggression towards others was because it helped me avoid needing help or needing anyone. If you get rid of all the people you love you will only have yourself to hate. I was okay with that. I didn't want to ever need someone and feel inferior or needy. I hate feeling inadequate and helpless. I did not want to need anyone and not have them reciprocate the love and affection I showed them.

The biggest disappointment I felt I had in life is loving people expecting them to love me the same way. The way things turned around for me was to just do things that I didn't want to do. Giving without expecting. Giving people the benefit of the doubt even if they were capable of failing. Loving others even if they didn't love me the same. I accepted a helping hand from the person that I believe God put in my life and trusted in God to see it through. That is what I learned from Jesh on top of so many other things.

In the book The Road Less Traveled, Dr. Scott Peck writes, "Whenever we seek to avoid the responsibility for our own behavior, we do so by attempting to give that responsibility to some other individual or organization or entity. But this means we then give away our power to that thing."

I'm glad that I had Jesh who was willing to stand up to my stubbornness. I'm glad I had a lawyer that wasn't afraid to tell me like it is. Always having things my way when I wanted them corrupted my true character and made me forget who I truly was destined to be. Looking back, I played the victim mentality so well that I didn't fit into the real world. I was living with the survivor mentality that prisoners adopt. I was like my old cell mate who blamed all the drama and troubles in life on someone else for the way things turned out. Blaming someone else for him getting busted.

There are things that you can't help. I get it. There are experiences that occurred which we are powerless over that live and breathe trauma in us. The experiences that give others that power over us. For instance, the abuse at every level in homes. I am not minimizing it or down playing it. I don't have the magic or flowery words to help you over that but I do pray you find the courage to overcome it. I'm pretty sure we all know others that have had similar experiences get through it and let God turn it around to become great successes for them. People who have probably gone through far worse. I have seen people let past abuse eat them alive until the pain was too much to manage and they ended up in bad places.

I know this first hand because I have a brother that drank and would hate that he was given the task of babysitting me. My brother was just a teen and I was younger. I was about 5 years old. My brother would be drinking with his friends outside our house and hate that he'd have to leave his lame friends or party to make sure I wasn't burning the house down. Which being troublesome, I was prone to do.

In order to allay any fears of me doing this, he'd try to force me to go to sleep. He thought that putting a young kid to sleep early would allow him the free time that he was due, to drink and enjoy the company of his friends. When he was drinking, it was always bad for me. The troubling thing about him was that he was always drinking.

My brother used to come in the room to check on me and see if I was sleeping. He'd punch me to see if I was up. He'd kick the head of the blanket when I was covered to see if I was really asleep. He'd torment me later if I told my Mom. These bad experiences had a controlling, traumatic effect on me to where it would push me back into the victim mind state every time I saw him drinking even as we got older. The response was different though because I was grown. I was angry. I would plot in my head smashing my brother's face in with a weapon when he passed out drunk. Watching him drinking uncontrollably, made me feel guilty for loving him but wanting him dead. Some of us can stay stagnant in fear and hate because of these types of experiences.

For a long time, I blamed my parents for leaving me alone with my brothers at such a young age. I blamed my brothers for the continuous assaults and beatings as a kid. I blamed myself for being too young and problematic that I would need supervision from someone only a few years older than me. The endless list goes on and on. So, when it came time to change and give up old behaviors I found that I wasn't ready. I wasn't willing. I was still mad at the world and couldn't allow myself to ever be a victim again. I couldn't see the pattern and how this led to being convicted of murder at the age of 13, nearly killing another guy at 19, and attacking prison guards at 26, and terrorizing the streets with guns blazing.

Unfortunately, I allowed this traumatic experience to make the mean-spirited person and defensive meanness my identity throughout adulthood. Being violent and aggressive because I experienced abuse led me down a dark path. I thought I was angry at life. But in truth, I was really afraid. Afraid that I would be put in this helpless situation again where I felt emasculated and weak. I was afraid that people would see me as a weakling and take advantage of me continuously. I adopted a survivor mentality that I needed to do unto others before they did unto me. I needed to prove that I wasn't someone to mess with by showing force and aggression at every opportunity. It took a long time for me to realize that I stunted my willingness and growth because I had allowed my pain to continue hurting me years and years after I had outgrown the events of my past. Hurt people hurt people. That's what I ended up being, a wounded and fearful soul. Hurtful and violent.

When I got sober and promised to do things differently, it was a huge contrast from what I was used to. Especially going to prison as a changed man. Adopting a new identity as a recovering alcoholic who just denounced and severed all ties with the biggest Samoan gang in the United States and one of the biggest crip sets in the world, which I had a leadership role in for years, wasn't very healthy for someone facing a lot of prison time. In fact, it was quite dangerous.

CHAPTER FIFTEEN

I went into a federal prison and started a bible study group of 13 members in a small two-man cell. I got active in recovery and became a representative for our group. I played drums for the inmate church. I started sponsoring guys, one of which would throw himself down the stairway so he could get pain meds from the medical staff. And more amazingly, I went through almost eight years without having any major infractions. Far different from me going in before without having any faith or recovery. The only two infractions I got were minor, and they were for hanging my towel off my bunk and for missing a psychology appointment.

I know that I had no hand in my being safe. In an environment like that, being from what I was from, going in alongside others from my gang that were also part of a nationwide conspiracy indictment, as a "changed man" wasn't the smartest thing to do. It did not matter, however. I had to be true to myself. I had to abandon full control and just trust in the creator which hadn't failed me yet. I remember an old timer telling me his story about giving up control before I got incarcerated. He'd tell me:

> *I used to try and control everything. I was obsessed with control. I was a control freak. I needed everything to be the way I wanted it to be and I would always find that things were more chaotic shortly after I tried to exert my will and power over it (funny because this is the same results I was having in wanting everything the way I wanted them when I wanted it). It wasn't until I Let Go absolutely, that I found things fell into place better than I could've wanted. It wasn't until I let God take control of everything that for some reason or the other everything fell into place. I had to truly let go to be in control.*

He would go on to tell me why the SERENITY prayer is so powerful.

> *God, grant me the serenity to accept the things that I cannot change. The courage to change the things I can. And the wisdom to know the difference. I didn't know the difference between what I did and did not have control over. I had a daughter that had not talked to me for years. I tried to control that relationship and it pushed her further and further away from me. I finally let go and let God. One day she called me and said she was getting married. She was extending this invitation to be present but not be noticed. She said she didn't want me to make any kind of attempt to be noticed. So, I went to her wed-*

ding and painfully watched as another man walked her down the aisle. I left when people started to take notice I was there.

I had a puzzled look on my face, and he continued.

A few months passed before my daughter called me again. She said she was pregnant. She was inviting me to show up at the hospital if she gave birth, but again, didn't want me to start buying things and doing things to be noticed. When she had her baby, I showed up at the hospital. I watched my grandson from a window. I left when her husband's family and friends showed up. I knew by her look that she was ready for me to leave. A few months later, she called to see if I'd be willing to take the baby for a few hours. I was ecstatic. Delighted. I babysat my grandson and am still doing so almost every day.

I was starting to be happy for him when he went on to finish his story.

My daughter died of an overdose. She was suffering from postpartum depression so bad that she started experimenting with pills. I can't help but to think that all the stress she felt about me compiled with all the stress she was already dealing with added to her depression. But I can't live like that. Unbalanced and trying to balance things out with the thoughts of "what-if's".

Trust that I learned a lot about trying to control the balance of life that day. I learned that I had to be willing to let go absolutely. That I had to be trusting, which I had never been in my life. I was so untrusting of anything that if people told me there was a light at the end of the tunnel I'd always think, yeah, it's an oncoming train.

I used to drive an hour out of town twice or three times a week with Jesh, come back and pay the bridge toll, all to get to the meeting that became my home group. We didn't have money. The feds seized most of my assets but followed me to meetings like I stashed it. They showed up to my speaking engagements and stood out like sore thumbs sitting in the back row. They looked like men in black or the bad guys in the matrix and were the only people wearing black suits and sunglasses in a nighttime meeting.

It was Jesh who pointed them out to me indicating that they were Feds. Funny because I could normally spot them a mile away. One night while they were trying to talk about recovery with me, Jesh rudely interrupted by asking, "Hey, what's your guys' home group?"

The Feds gave us some bogus answer. Jesh looked it up and it was non-existent. He asked them for the address. They gave him one to a Walmart warehouse. He pulled me away and showed me the results on his phone and I left the Feds standing there looking all matrix in the middle of a recovery crowd.

Well, they say in recovery, "If you have decided you want what we have and are willing to go to any lengths to get it, then you are ready to take these certain steps." I'm going to be real with you. I didn't go to all that length to have what they had. I was going to any lengths to NOT have what I had. What I had was killing me. I didn't want or know what other people in recovery had. I was still suspicious of people and telling myself, remember not everyone in church is a saint. And not everyone in recovery is working the program. The thing is, my home group was suspicious of me too. They would approach me before the meeting and ask me to surrender my pistol before they were comfortable with me going in. They did this to me a couple times. When I went to the gunman selling "throw aways" in my city to get a new gun, he'd say, "Man, remind me never to piss you off." He thought I was out shooting people and throwing away the evidence. Hence the name "throw aways." I lived in Tacoma, so of course I needed a pistol. What? My faith wasn't as strong then.

If you are thinking of getting involved in recovery or are new to it, I want you to know that that weird feeling is natural. I was actually weirded out my first time going to meetings or going inside churches. I wasn't used to people coming up and telling me, "We're going to love you until you love yourself." I had the sweetest old lady named Carol come up to me telling me that at my first meeting and it spooked me. People made me paranoid. I never had someone do something good for me just to do it. There were always strings of selfish reasoning behind it. I was afraid of people who said they loved me. I was afraid of love is what it really boiled down to. I didn't know how they could be genuinely happy. It was somewhat disturbing because I wanted to be happy like they were but DID NOT believe it was possible. We always think, oh yeah, it can happen for others but not for us. I don't know why that is. It's like we are always going to seminars, or shrinks, and doctors, to tell us what we already know to be true because we don't trust ourselves to be right. Like we can't be right about things that we know should be for us. Like we are not lovable, worthy, or deserving for some reason.

I'm going to tell you a story about this tech friend of mine named Steve to explain what I mean. I was always that kid outside looking in, never a part of, always apart from. This friend Steve, I believe, felt the same way. Our unfriendly and antisocial attitude made life easier to deal with. We medicated ourselves through the negative process of isolation that it became a source of healing. We pushed people away by saying, "You wouldn't understand." And when people left us alone, we got the greatest dose of DontBotherMe-naprine at 1,500 milligrams a shot. Keeping people at bay, in fear of trying to clarify things, but making them worse, is just easier. Somehow me and Steve managed to make a strong connection through a common interest.

The truth is, he and I, like a lot of us addicts, don't play well with others. We enjoy the discomfort of being alone. We enjoy isolation. But no one really wants to be alone. We just did not know how to communicate our thoughts and feelings in a way that is not offensive and destructive to relationships. Consequently, we opt out and isolate instead of putting up the effort to change. If this is you, look up "Adverse Child Experience" and how the more you act on it the more it affects and damages your social and human development. ACE, as it is known, is one of the root causes for kids growing up with instability, bonding, and insecurity issues. Studies find that growing up having Adverse Childhood Experiences makes you more susceptible to substance abuse, mental health issues, and even lead to prison.

When I first began my path to change, I started to extend my friendship to anyone who needed a friend. I found what bands us together as a people is having a common interest. I have since tried to repair a lot of the relationships I've damaged or destroyed upon learning this, but some people would not have it. You are responsible for putting in the effort and how much you are willing to give that relationship though. In every relationship it takes two people to make it work. It can't be reliant on one person doing all the heavy lifting. I've seen toxic relationships turn healthy and healthy relationships turn toxic. In the end, it is the efforts that people put into their relationship that results in either success or failure for them.

Through the program of recovery, I've found friends that show up for me like I show up for them. Being stunted emotionally, as I said, not wanting to hear what anyone had to say was crippling. It made me reliant on what I knew only, and not open minded or receptive to information that would've helped me grow. This is what stopped me from learning, which in turn, stopped me from growing. You know this type, the ones that are not active listeners because they only hear to form a response but not to listen. Men that are grown and gray and still act like children with arrested development issues. Guys that haven't really grown up because they were locked away trapped in time. The result of not actively getting involved in schooling programs or challenging yourself when you are away, can lead to this without you knowing. I've seen this characteristic trait in my friends who would rather work on building their outward appearance through exercise and weights instead of their inward identity and mind. The hope is that they will meet someone that admires them for their looks and be interested enough to take care of them. Unsurprisingly, there is a world of women waiting to fill that void. Insecurities, attention, adventure, a need to exercise their maternal nature by taking care of someone, (bored housewives) all show up to visiting time in prison.

I got married and divorced in prison to a girl who was a higher up in a power company. I dated a psych doctor working for Social Security, a Legal Assistant, a financial advisor, and a Corporate Lawyer (not all at the same time) all while serving time in prison. So, I know. They were in love with the image that is not my identity. When they realized I couldn't reach the expectation or standard they had set extremely too high for me, they left. I learned and realized later in life it had nothing to do with me in terms of their attraction to prison guys.

Back to this friend of mine, Steve. He grew up with wealthy parents and had everything that money can buy. His parents were part of the tech start-up era in Washington in the early 90's and both became successful in their careers. They both graduated from top tech schools and soon enough became part of two tech businesses that would emerge out of the northwest as two of the biggest tech companies in the world. Amazon and Microsoft. This kid had it all or at least that's what I thought. Steve was a genius in his own right. By the time he was ten, he was writing his own codes for games. He was multilingual in computer languages. He could code in pascal, perl, python, C++, and many more. When it came to computers, he was brilliant.

I met him in Junior college my first year and wondered why this kid never went to a prestigious University or Ivy League school. I mean surely his parents could afford it. They were probably major donors to a lot of them. It later dawned on me that this kid, even with all the wealth he came from, with all the opportunity and resources available to him, wasn't happy with who his parents expected him to be. He didn't want to follow in their footsteps and chose his own path. His own identity. He wanted to be adventurous and pursued his own dreams. He became a well-known black hat hacker on the internet and was responsible for some famous malicious hacking tools that script kiddies (people who are not real hackers that buy hacker tools off the darkweb from coders) used to hack huge companies. He, like most hackers I'd meet in life, loved the isolation and politicking of keeping people at bay. They love their dark corner of the world behind a computer and a modem where they can access any part of the world through code.

When I first met him, his hustle was writing term papers for kids struggling through college. I didn't know he was also experimenting with making fake I.D.s at the time and was known for taking tests on behalf of students. Yes, he had it down to a science. He was also cloning credit cards and living like a kid that didn't come from money. Well one day, I found Steve being bullied and getting beat on by some kids. Me being bigger and tougher, thought I could easily negotiate a peaceful resolution with these kids but I was wrong. I had to demonstrate the level of violence I found necessary in life when communicating with people who only understood violence.

Shortly after the incident, Steve and I became fast friends. Unbeknownst to me, he was doing what he does and that the kids beating up on him were trying to extort him into writing their paper and doing their homework without pay. Unbeknownst to him, I was doing what I did which was selling dope and beating up kids that didn't pay. Soon, he was asking if I needed help and would help me with my schooling, but I never allowed him to do my papers for me. I felt that it would be a waste of time. I wasn't interested in his skills. I wanted to develop my own. Unlike the other kids in school that just wanted to party and sleep through class, but still pass with flying colors, I was in it for the education. I wasn't in it for the piece of paper to hang as a plaque on the wall like I earned it.

Steve got us job interviews for AT&T. He had taken care of setting up the interviews through his parents and took care of the interview pre-screening test by hacking into it. This was my first job ever fresh out of youth prison and it was amazing to be young and making a lot of money at 19 years old. The thing about Steve was, he wasn't naïve. He picked up quickly what I was involved in and soon became interested. Meanwhile I only thought him capable of writing term papers.

When he learned of the drug trade, he was fascinated with it and wanted the attention that came with it. For a guy who was a loner, he sure did yearn to be loved and admired, adored and wanted. Explaining to him that people didn't really love me and adore me, they only valued me because what I provided. It was like trying to explain to a blind man what driving was like. I told him to watch how people acted when I said I didn't have anything, as opposed to when I told them I did. I don't know why I thought this would end discussion as the best argument, but it didn't. I couldn't get through to him. He kept insisting he wanted to be part of that world.

This guy wrote programs that would help me with my work while we were both employed by AT&T Broadband and Internet Service at the time, and these programs would cut my workload from eight hours to one hour. I spent most of the time at work walking around and goofing off, pretending to be busy. I never understood what fascinated him about drug dealing. As I look back on everything, I wish I took full advantage of that position to really learn the trade and become legit. I was too young and dumb to understand the value in working for the largest cell phone company in the world, with service products like cable, radio, and broadband and internet services.

Steve created an app (before cell phone apps were even popular) that would spam bomb a phone number. I would put all the drug dealers in my neighborhood's numbers on this program and it would blow their phone up by calling them back to back. When they answered their phone it would hang up, and when they hung up it would call them back. But every time the program called the phone, it would change the number to spoof a number out of their contacts. It was genius. It was also very illegal. The drug dealers wouldn't be able to use their phones because it was being bombarded with calls. Because of this, they'd have to call someone else when they needed to resupply and the one person they knew by heart was mine. I could offload whatever I picked up at the time because I had more demand than I had supply. I wasn't trying to take on selling fulltime because I really was interested in school. I didn't have the credentials and financial backing this kid had.

A serious associate approached me with a proposition one day that involved Steve's hacker abilities. He wanted Steve to start cashing out huge loans, taxes, insurance checks and whatever else. Steve was excited at the prospect of getting involved with hacking on a much larger scale. I was opposed to it. I was the voice of reason trying to get him to weigh the pros and cons. Lo and behold, he went on to become one of the biggest, if not the biggest, credit card and fraud guys in the town. Soon enough he was taking his show on the road and traveling the country. Steve linking up with this associate of mine got him hooked on meth. He was in denial when I saw him again and said that he was just smoking in order to stay up and do what he loved. Hacking. A lot of the best hackers I knew at the time were addicted to some form of drug, so I understood. I could see my friend spiraling downward however, and wanted him to start reconsidering his life choices. It was apparent he was imploding. His identity was fast becoming that of a person who was only needed for his services but not loved for his person.

Trying to tell him about his addictions while suffering from my own, was like trying to teach a blind man to sail a boat while we're on the front end of it, while the back end was half way in the water. Not long after I last saw him, Steve was wanted by law enforcement for a string of charges. Word was that his identity he built made him a wanted man and gave him a lot more attention than he wanted. As fate would have it, he was said to be the victim of a fatal hit and run tragedy that ended his life. My fondest memory of my friend is reminiscent of when he'd always use these blind man analogies to try to explain things to me. In the end, he didn't see what I was trying to warn him about all along and was blinded by his ambitions. I always told him that love is someone not needing nothing from you, but you.

It's crazy because years later while in prison, a guy was walking by my cell with a tech magazine that had Steve's uncle's picture on the front cover. I borrowed the magazine and read about a famous tech icon who was Steve's uncle. His uncle's pictures were all over Steve's house, and Steve told me that it's who he was named after. I remembered the pictures but couldn't believe how famous his uncle was. His uncle was none other than Steve Jobs, the founder of Apple.

Finding yourself is not just difficult in recovery, but in life in general. It is why gangs had such a strong lure on me because it gave me a false sense of belonging. They made me feel like I was an integral part of something bigger than myself. They made me feel like I was loved. Understanding the need for validation and desire for attention is what helped me change. I think the most trivial pursuit in life is striving to be someone you're not, only to find out it's something that you're stuck with, and it doesn't make you happy. It's like getting a tattoo to fit in, making a big purchase to be seen, or getting married to someone for the sake of doing so, and later regretting it. I'm just saying that I've known people who chose a career path and spent years pursuing it only to get to middle aged and want something entirely different. Yet in their initial pursuit of their career, they said it was what they love doing. I know you can't see me, but I have my hand raised as one of those people.

I grew up wanting to be like my brothers and grandpa who were infamously known for their violent nature, but it wasn't me. I had misperceived my purpose and furthermore misjudged incorrectly what I thought others purposes were. I misperceived other's roles based on what I believe were their weaknesses and strengths, what I believe their limited capabilities were. For this, I blamed myself for my friend for a long time. I had people tell me that had it not been for me, he'd have given himself over to that life anyway. That was inevitable. But nah. He was a good kid and I was the catalyst to his downfall. He might not have ever known anyone deeply involved with drugs and crime to take him to where my associates took him. No excuse.

SAVAGE RECOVERY

Matthew 6:9-13

9 Our Father which art in heaven, Hallowed be thy name.

10 Thy kingdom come, Thy will be done on earth, as it is in heaven.

11 Give us this day our daily bread.

12 And forgive us our debts, as we forgive our debtors.

13 And lead us not into temptation, but deliver us from evil: For thine is the kingdom, and the power, and the glory, forever. Amen.

CHAPTER SIXTEEN

In psychology, they define insanity as doing the same thing over and over and expecting different results. What's insane to me is people who get out of prisons, jail, institutions or addictions, get good paying jobs, the house, the spouse, everything they never thought possible, and then go back to active using even years after having their lives almost fully restored in sobriety. They go back to the very thing that broke them. They go back to the life they worked so very hard to get away from. They go back to the one very thing that caused them pain, misery, and suffering like they have never known otherwise in their lives.

I've had this experience from time to time in my life where I'd compromise, sabotage, or deliberately destroy any success or opportunity I had because I didn't feel worthy of success, or worthy of good things. Like I said, I could often see something good as a fit for someone else but not for myself. I couldn't identify it while in the process of self-sabotage, but it did make sense to me later in therapy and recovery. I learned that my rash way of thinking was causing me to do the same things over and over and expecting results. This irrational and distorted way of thinking was called thinking errors. It played a huge role in my mental lapses and poor judgment.

For those of you that don't know what thinking errors are, they are cognitive distortions in our thinking that are irrational and inaccurate. Learning what they are will help you change the way you think, which in turn will have you change the way you live.

Ten of the most common thinking errors are:

Overgeneralizing – Having one bad experience with a cop and now thinking that all cops are bad.

All-or-Nothing – Everything is black and white with no room for gray areas. You look at things in a way that I used to, which reinforced my distorted beliefs and thoughts for politicking. "I might as well be bad because that's what everyone thinks I am anyway."

Catastrophizing – This was one of my favorites. Making things seem worse than they really are. For example, if the police show up at my door unannounced, I think assumptively, "Oh no, someone close to me died in a car wreck," or "YOU'RE NOT TAKING ME ALIVE COPPERS!!! I know you found something from my past that can put me away for life." When in reality, they could be just going door-to-door warning neighbors to lock their cars because of recent break-in reports.

Negative Filtering – You have nine good things going your way but if one thing doesn't, that is what you focus all your attention and time on.

Fortune Telling – In recovery they call this future tripping; "They are not going to hire me with all these felonies I got so I'm just not going to go to the interview and waste my time."

Unreal Deal – Making comparisons between yourself and others. "I'm looking at 20 years in prison while Purdue Pharma lied about opioids being addictive, which killed good innocent people, paying off large fines in settlements, and they get to go scot-free?"

Labeling – Putting names to people that reinforces a negative vibe. Calling cops "pigs" reinforced my belief that they were all bad, yet I met more good cops than bad ones.

Mind Reading – "That guy's staring at me because he has a problem with me." When, really, the guy is admiring your necklace.

Personalizing – If someone doesn't say hi to you they must not like you. You focus on that one person and think they are mad at you. You let this one person not saying hi ruin your entire day when really, that person's probably going through their own issue that doesn't involve you or they simply didn't notice you.

Emotional Reasoning – Letting my emotions get the best of me was one of my downfalls. I'd base things on emotions and use this reasoning, which deprived myself of a fair chance at many opportunities. "I feel like I don't relate to people at the meetings so I'll stay away from it." I don't relate to anyone there.

Knowing what thinking errors are now, you should be able to readily identify most of them in my story growing up or identify them in your own battle with recovery. One of my default thinking errors was catastrophizing. Always assuming things were worse than they really are and using all the supporting assumptions to make them so. In my case, as a kid, it almost seemed like the worst always happened, so I began feeling like the worst was always yet to come. In recovery, they teach you about "stinking thinking," and how it affects your character. This is something I couldn't see when surrounding myself with those that use thinking errors or encouraged and enabled mine. I recall how I thought I could fix things myself through my strong will and intellectual nature when I realized the problem, but I couldn't.

I'd tell myself, "Okay, this time I'm just going to 'program' and stay out the way. I'm just going to enroll in educational studies and stay busy by being positive. I'm going to live and let live and avoid prison politics."

Yet my distorted thinking always allowed something or someone to get me angry. My irrational way of thinking always got me into some mess. A broken brain can't fix a broken brain, no matter how much mental awareness I had. It was only when I found recovery and got sober, that I learned a new way of thinking that helped me cope with the feeling of unworthiness, being short tempered, feeling needy, and so on. It was only through therapeutic recovery that I saw my flaws and errors in thinking and got me excited about the possibility of change. I found matters of the mind so intriguing that I was eager to understand more. Like a guy who won the lottery, I made sure to attend every meeting and session because it was a huge win for me. If someone told you that you won the mega lottery, that all you had to do was pick it up, it wouldn't matter if the office to claim your winnings were on the moon, you would find a way to get there. That is how I felt when I'd drive for hours, out of town, to the meetings I attended.

Even after getting out sober this time, I had to be mindful of these things. I had to tell myself this over and over, mentally beating this into my own head to be aware of the pitfalls of my thinking. I had to drum the emphasis of it in my brain, that prison should never be the consequence of my pursuit of happiness or my desire for financial stability. I had to fully concede to my innermost self that destruction, prison, relapse, and all else that leads me backwards is not an option no matter what. I had to realize that no one could make me angry, upset, mad, furious, or happy. That it was my irrational and inaccurate way of seeing things that was leading me to so freely give away that power to others. Knowing this about me made me aware of how much I needed a power greater than myself to help. I couldn't do this alone. I had to be mindful that my thoughts needed to be based on facts and objectivity, which kept my emotions in check. I could have told myself these things over and over before, until I was blue in the face, promised myself all I wanted to, and nothing would have changed had it not been for the reliance on something greater than myself. I had to do the steps again or die.

I know that many people thought that the book would be about my life. The drunk-a-log and my partying. Well, my story is not any different from any story you've already heard from any drunk around the way. Reliving those times in the pages of my life today is not something I wanted to focus on. Even if my relationship with alcohol didn't always take a dark turn after drinking, it still wasn't worth mentioning. Deric used to say, "Not every time I drank something bad would happen, but every time something happened, I was drinking."

Well, for me, something bad almost always happened. There's nothing really to tell about my life that is different from a lot of people in recovery other than I probably had more friends with Saturday morning cartoon names. My best friend who I started my alcoholic and criminal career with was kid they called Gargamel. Yes, the character from the Smurf cartoon. Gargamel had triangle scars on his face that that three circle shapes in them from his stepdad taking a hot iron to it. What can I say? Our childhoods weren't filled with a recollection of fond memories other than we drank and formed a bond through gang activities. We survived the streets by breaking the laws, and the only useful thing I remember being known for was crime.

Recently, a guy at work locked his keys in his car. Everyone was out there trying to get the door unlocked and be named the hero for the day. They were doing more damage than good to this guy's car. My boss says, "Call Mani. He can open this car without leaving a scratch." I opened it. No scratch.

When I first got sober, it was Deric who taught me about a wide variety of alcoholic types from A through Z. A-types, he taught, are the ones that are starting out experimenting and drinking occasionally. Then there are B-types, the ones that are beyond experimenting and are finding that they do it more than occasional. C-types are the ones that are functioning and hanging in there; they go to work but find that they are drinking daily. All the way down to the Z-types. These types are powerless over it altogether and they find themselves living under the bridge and giving up all hope.

They drink all day everyday if possible. I say this because many alcoholics/addicts start out thinking that they are not at all bad because they haven't reached their bottoms yet. They say to themselves, "I'll never get to that point." However, they don't realize that many of the Z-types started off as the A-types.

When Deric taught me this, I had gotten to the stage of my drinking where I wasn't fun to drink with. I'd call friends to meet up for a drink and they'd all make excuses that they were spending time with their wives, or they had something important to do the next day. Thinking I would probably not go out, I'd go to the bars and see all of them there. I was in a place where no one wanted to be around me. Heck, I didn't want to be around me, but I couldn't bring myself to stop. Guys' wives were even telling them that they needed to stay away from me. The amazing thing is one of these same wives that said to stay away from me told my friend to call me when she found out I was sober. I took that friend to the Step Workshop with Deric and Ted and that was all he wrote. He was surprised about having six months sober when he did. He didn't feel like it was real. I ended up being his sponsor and it was weird because I knew this guy's secrets without him having to tell me. I knew his sins before he shared. I knew things that haunted him because he was part of my crew running the streets with me before sobriety. He had almost a year sober before the streets came calling him back and he relapsed.

CHAPTER SEVENTEEN

What's so different with me? I had to ask myself. What's so different with you? I would ask guys who've reached out to me to find out what I've been doing to change and what I've done to maintain that staying power. I asked this because I wanted to get to the bottom of why it was good for someone who celebrated recovery after 20 years, but we would think it was impossible for us. I would ask guys from prison who called. I would say that they would need to change the one thing that I did. That one thing being EVERYTHING. Guys would hang up and never call me again. I get it. There are things they weren't ready to give up in their lives in order to live joyous and free.

I remember the first time I went into treatment and they asked on the questionnaire, how often does a normal person get drunk? I was in denial. Me, wanting to ace this in-take form and sound like I wasn't an alcoholic, I started calculating and applying my prison math because I was going to wow the counselors. I would think, okay, well there's Christmas, Thanksgiving, and New Year. So, that's three guaranteed. There's a birthday party in there somewhere. So, that's four. Not wanting to seem alcoholic, I said, "A good six times is average." The counselor was wowed alright. Disappointingly, you know what I found out? I was dead wrong. Normal people don't get drunk. They can stop when they want to. I remembered being annoyed at being wrong and at all the normal people for always ruining everything.

I thought about my ex-girlfriend Amy. I always got mad at her because she'd go with me to a party and not feel the need to drink. If she did, she could have a sip and leave her drink unfinished when we left. It bugged me. I felt like it was a waste of time and money. Why go to a party where there is drinking and not drink? It was like going to a swimming pool where there is swimming and not swim. Or just going to the swimming pool to dip your toe in the water. You can tell by that last statement that I struggled through my early years of recovery. I know many guys coming home think of meetings as treatment or rehab. Well, it's nothing like it. Completely the opposite. They say this is a program for people that want it, not for people that need it. Many people will die because they don't want it enough or themselves.

I had so many mixed emotions and irrational thoughts that I had to identify and get rid of to get sober and stay sober the second time around. Some of which were deeply guarded thoughts that were roots of my beliefs, and feelings that were roots of my emotional trauma. Being in the right environment where they facilitated the deep digging into your soul is the only thing, I know worked for me. You must think, I came from all the pain and hurt that I laid out and I can tell you that's not even the tip of it. If this works for me though, I know it can work for anyone. That environment I'm describing isn't some fancy, huge treatment center with offices and posters of recovery all over. Nah, it was a little room where drunks gathered and shared the truths from the bottoms of their souls.

Recovery accompanied by therapy taught me that we, as alcoholics/addicts, carry tons of emotional baggage everywhere we go. It's amazing how in recovery and therapy I came to discover that I had stockpiled guilt and shameful memories, in the deepest part of my soul, yet was the biggest scaredy cat when it came time to confront them. My sponsor's pitch on the steps was the same way trauma can affect you for years is the same way recovery can help you in life, but positively.

The steps gave me anxiety. The problem I had with the steps is what many newcomers struggle with. Strangers want to dig into your thousand-ton pile of dirty laundry. And you're not supposed to feel judged at all? I didn't even know about in-depth guilt and shame prior to recovery. I came to learn that I was carrying a ton of emotional baggage of junk that I towed around with me through life in recovery. My sponsor told me that the toxicity of this baggage was what was corroding my mind and festering venomous poisons inside my heart. Yet, I lived with it from a young age and although it turned me insanely miserable, I was afraid to confront it. I was told that confronting this part of my life was going to make me helpful rather than hurtful to others. It didn't make any sense to me as a newcomer. I would argue, "Some of us are hoarders. We like our thousand-ton pile of dirty laundry without someone pointing out our dirty underwear and socks." An argument that always fell on deaf ears with my sponsor.

In all honesty though, the weight of my sins when I came to recovery was anchoring me down and holding me under an ice-cold river. It kept me captive by impairing my movement and my progress to breathe normally. That negative pile of junk is what formed my evil character and my bad identity. I had to unload all of it and remove the clutter to truly know what true freedom felt like. Still, I was scared. The liberation from this junk and evil was one of the greatest feelings I ever felt, but I didn't know that just coming in. I will tell you that there is no other relief like getting through this part of recovery. The peace I felt is like no other. It was like that feeling that had me kicking and screaming in the SHU, eventually busting my toe. I kid you not, I could literally feel myself becoming lighter in the weeks and months that followed after having dumped this weight and burden, that it was like I was walking on air. This is the thing though, I had to work the program. Not my program, not my sponsor's program, but THE program. I had to do the steps with that 'one' which we run from like avoiding the plague, which is the most gratifying and rewarding of them all if you get through it. I came to find that this single step has been the make or break all and has been responsible for more lives changing in the alcoholic/ addict community than anything else. Same one responsible for more newcomers falling off than COVID. If you know you know. You probably are hoping I don't say it. But, yes, the Fourth Step: Making a fearless and moral inventory of yourself.

 Look, I know! I had grave secrets I swore that I would never tell a living soul. I had gang secrets that I took a vow to protect with my life. Crimes on top of crimes. Sins on top of sins. Dirt on top of dirt. Heck, I had things that have eaten me alive since I was a young kid. I mean, all these secrets kept me living a 'crooked' life like I was suffering from a spinal injury. And just like an injury that healed improperly, and we'd prefer to live with the deformity than suffer the pain of reopening that wound to correct it, I had to be broken to be healed. I remember avoiding the process of freedom through the steps initially, like a train seeing the fourth step and jumping off tracks to take the shortcut dirt roads. Yes, I was like everyone who is a skeptic about this ever working. In a sense, it was a huge decision to make. It was really like a life changing surgical procedure. Except maybe this one is spiritual. I can't explain how it works but I will tell you though, it truly does.

They say in recovery that you have to learn to "live life on life's terms," and the confessions of the soul, I believe, is the most empowering act that has helped a lot of people in the program find peace and serenity. It has helped me find peace. If you think about it, confessions are nothing new. Catholics have done it in confessional booths. Patients seeing shrinks do it in therapy. People that have admitted to their guilt have been liberated and freed even inside of prison in their captive spaces. The truth will set you free. I don't know why but it's worked for millions of others in and outside of recovery. My grand sponsor used to say, "You know, I never got away with anything. God was always watching." Meaning he could never hide his shame and guilt, so confronting them was the only option he had.

I don't know if this helps you, but the same old timer, Ted, that used to say how alcoholism is like diarrhea it runs in your "jeans," used to also say, "Once you get over telling on yourself about sleeping with the farm animals and with your siblings, and whatever plastic doll there is in your story, the rest will come out easily." We are only as sick as our deepest secrets, they say in recovery. I grew up hush hush. If anyone knew about secrets it was me. I had secrets on top of secrets. I didn't want anyone to know the true me. No one does want to be vulnerable like that.

"You won't heal it if you don't reveal it," I heard a Christian radio host say on the air one day. A doctor can't help you if you don't tell him what's wrong with you. This is why I broke my book up into three parts. These parts have nothing to do with stages or phases of recovery but I felt it should be talked about. One being of the mind, one of the body, and the last being of the spirit. These secrets keep the spirit sick and broken. We have to free our spirit before we can free ourselves from our addictions, Finding spirituality in recovery may be challenging for someone new so I wanted to share what it was like for me.

Many newcomers find themselves not feeling like they belong because they have their core beliefs that keeps them politicking. Seeing the world with a shady pair of glasses keeps us from opening up. Many of them not understanding their identity, still wanting to fill that void with outside attention and admiration. It is why social media is so popular. The pleasure center portion of the brain gets triggered every time we get likes and hearts on our pictures or posts. Getting likes and hearts releases the same chemicals in our brain that alcohol and drugs do in our system. Dopamine and serotonin. Absent in the minds of the spiritually immature newcomer though, is that you can't purchase the feeling of acceptance, nor can you find it on social media. You can't fill this void with materialistic or superficial likes and hearts. Savage recovery is the spirit in this equation. It's the encouragement to take action. The motivation to rise and run with it. Like I said before, recovery is way more than just about being abstinent from drugs and alcohol.

It's also about forgiveness of the haunting past.

It's about letting go of things which causes you those recurring nightmares and sleepless nights.

It's about fighting off a traumatic experience that victimized you as a child; Adverse Child Experiences that prompt you to become a serial violator acting out illegal behaviors because you can't bring yourself to get through the balancing acts of life.

It's about being a conqueror of tragic events and grievous issues you've experienced and been exposed to.

Recovery is overcoming your demons and exposing them to the sun, in order to climb out of that darkness you are in. It's about learning to peacefully coexist with others who hurt you without wanting to go and exact revenge on them wherever they may be.

It's about serenity.
It's about Peace.
It's about Tranquility.
Redemption.
Growth.
It's about strength.

It's about taking the power back from everything that drains you mentally, emotionally, and spiritually, and giving the power back to God. It's about understanding that it's okay not to be okay. But also understanding you're can't stay there. Acknowledging where you are in life is one thing, but recognizing where you are and knowing that there's more to come and more to you than past decisions and mistakes is an entirely different thing. There's more to you than your flaws. There's more to you than pain. Coming to terms and knowing that I'm not where I want to be, but I'm definitely not where I used to be, is growth. If you are a recovering alcoholic or addict, I suggest to you the steps. Stairway to Heaven!

"It's only a mistake if you don't correct it." This was a saying that one teacher in the Hawaii Youth Corrections used to tell me. In the Hawaii Youth Correctional Facility, they made you go to school because it is the law. It is mandatory. I was in a special reading class and I hated it because I knew I was different. I would act out violently towards teachers and staff that were trying to teach me to read. One teacher took me outside one day and confronted me about my ill behavior. She asked, "What's the problem? Is it my breath? Is it something to do with me?"

I told her, "I can't read!"

She kept explaining to me that she was there to help me learn to read. I spit in her face and was sent to the SHU.

Another teacher asked me to read out loud one day. Because I didn't know how to read, I got up and took the spinning globe model she had in class and bashed her head with it. I didn't know it was made of cardboard but the globe split in half. I was sent to the SHU.

This teacher though, unlike any other teachers I've dealt with, showed up at my door with books in hand for me to read. The nerve. We talked about how she forgave me. She joked that the globe was made out of the same cardboard that the chicken in the prison was made of so she didn't hurt. It just made her hungry. She made fun of me saying that I needed a weapon against a woman, showing how much of a coward I was. With my head hanging down shamefully, I agreed.

When she first showed up at my cell door, I lashed out and kicked the door and I did stuff toddlers do when they are embarrassed. I tore the books that she would slide under the door and make paper planes out of the pages. Her strange sense of humor and bold toughness is what actually made me comfortable. I laughed at her jokes. She was really funny. She would read to me and try to persuade me to read a page or so. I refused. It was my great weakness – reading.

One day I was bored and I started reading with her as she stood at the door. All the books she had were Disney books that were for elementary children. But I read them with her while she was flipping pages on the other side of the door. Soon enough she'd leave me a book with the confidence that I wasn't making paper planes. And when she returned she wanted me to tell her all about it. Next. She wanted me to write down what I remembered from it like a book report. Before you knew it, I was reading out loud to her. Soon enough, I would attempt to read everything and anything I could get my hands on. Not just the books that she brought me. I wanted to read everything from soap boxes to shampoo bottles to actual encyclopedia size books.

Later, I was reading and actually understanding so much that I was infatuated with reading. I was addicted to it. I craved anything that had words, so much that I read the dictionary and recalled meanings, synonyms and antonyms for words. I couldn't contain the need to read. I'd devour novels in about two days. I consumed college textbooks in about four days. I read the Bible numerous times from front to back. The Qur'an. The Torah. Buddhist literature. This teacher was bringing me psychology books, philosophy books, law books, and every kind of book that the local university would donate to her. Before you knew it, me and her had developed a bond that is one of the strongest I ever felt to another human being. I fell in love with reading and it became the best mental escape ever. I could take a trip into the land of my imagination right there in my cell.

I would read through the night because in isolation I had nothing better to do. I started remembering passages. I started collecting quotes in my head. I fell in love with books like it was someone to love and adore. I started writing poems and she would enter these poems I had in little contests, and they would win, surprisingly. She was entering what I had written in writing circles and my writings became acknowledged. I did a charcoal drawing self-portrait, and it won a National Art Award Contest and was hung in the capitol in Washington D.C. I was awarded the *Kahekili* Art Award that year by the Lt. Governor of Hawaii all while being locked up in youth prison.

She entered me in a state essay contest on "Freedom" and I beat out so many kids from public and private schools that I won my actual freedom after the Honorable Judge Uale had learned about it. I was supposed to be sentenced to juvenile life until I turned 20 but because the judge saw that I had potential to think on my own, he granted me early release at age 19. Not only did this teacher help me in that respect, she also helped me win scholarships that would help pay my way through college, which she enrolled me in. This is how I ended up in the same junior college as my hacker friend Steve. I owe so much to this teacher and thank all teachers who go out of their way to give a kid a chance at life. She always told me I should write a book and I never considered it until now. I made a lot of mistakes in my past that I realized later, "It's only a mistake if you don't correct it."

Now I know people might be thinking, all that reading you did, and you didn't know God? Yup. Reading about spiritual things when I learned to read wasn't exactly real to me. They were fantasy reads. I was trying to understand it but never could. Parting of the Red Seas. Floods. Famines. War. I couldn't wrap my head around it. It was like there were things that I couldn't comprehend that kept me in disbelief. I only identified as Christian because recovery adopted so many Christian sayings and practices that I started going to church when I got sober. I don't know whether to thank God for recovery or to thank recovery for God. It took me coming to believe that I saw so many miracles that were beyond coincidence with people who I knew followed Christ. I'd be foolish to continue disbelieving. I think that my experience with church when I was young was what blocked me from the spirit. Oddly, being a pastor's son. I met many pastors' sons in prison, and it never occurred to me that we were probably the target of the adversary in our fathers' spiritual journey. You only know what you know.

There are things that defined me before. Things that I no longer identify with. There are things that may have defined you too, but you can change them by doing things differently now. Things that won't just affect you, it'll affect the community you live in and the world you leave behind. Things like service, work, and volunteering. Things like helping someone that can't pay you back. My sponsor used to say, "You are what you do. If you steal horses, you are a horse thief. If you steal cars, you are a car thief. But what if you gave all the horses back? Or what if you paid for all the cars you stole? You are no longer what you were." As part of the step work, I have earnestly tried to give back and correct my wrongs. Places that I've robbed, I've sent a check to, not explaining what I did wrong but just that I owed the. People I have hurt, I've reached out to make amends. And for those that I could never make amends to, I pray that my living change along with repentance will suffice one day.

Some people are okay with being sick when they get to this hard part of doing the steps. They prefer to stay in their sickness, in their secrets, so much so that they back out of recovery instead of going forward knowing this could help. It takes courage to change. I had fears too. I feared that my sponsor would tell others. I feared he'd look at me funny. I feared that someone would want both of us dead now and that I drug him into the mix by revealing to him secrets I shouldn't have. It is all fear. And fear is nothing more than what it really is – a stressor. If you look it up, you will see what I mean. It's a builder of cortisol and all kinds of other chemical parts of your body that in short, can kill you. It's what's been driving us nuts for years and holding us hostage if we live under its control. They say in recovery we suffer from a thousand forms of fear. I know it would be really ironic to come into recovery barely breathing, end up sober, only to die from the fear and stress of doing the steps. I'm happy to report that this hasn't happened yet. People that have died in recovery die of self-inflicted food comas and old age. In recovery they say that when fear knocks, faith answers, and there is no one there.

In truth, fear is not at all a bad thing. It's the part of our brain that helps us stay alive and survive. It helps us overcome a lot of our challenges if used as a motivator. The fight or flight response is how we avoid danger. Maybe not so much for me because I think I had my wires crossed and would charge towards danger like it's fun. I think a lot of alcoholic/addicts are trip-wired that way that we'd often find the dangerous thing appealing. Like finding the wrong mate, or the wrong situation to get involved in continuously and then have the nerve to blame it on bad luck when things fell apart. I was inspired by all the wrong things and took off like a 747 jet down the runway to get to it fast. It was just me being fearful and wanting to create a persona of crazy until eventually I couldn't tell the blurs in the line.

At first, when I heard people talk about motivation and willingness in recovery, it didn't make sense to me. In the process of changing, but not doing it quickly enough for others, they would tell me, "You lack the motivation. You lack willingness. You're lazy." I would think, "Nah, I just really don't have the intrigue or interest in it."

I think we are drawn to things that we are intrigued and interested in. Finding change and seeing recovery as simple for others, is harder for people like me because it takes a while to get involved. It's why I said it took someone like my brother Jesh or sponsor to get on me, which got me moving. I'd always argue that things like fighting or assaulting someone that bruised my little ego, didn't require motivation. I had it wired to immediately respond when I felt insulted or challenged. It's a wonder I relapsed. Intrigue and interest in recovery only came to be at the speed of light with my last desperation for oblivion and death.

I want to share a powerful story from this girl I knew as a child but we lost touch as adults. When we were kids she was not so good looking. She would always talk about one day she would be on T.V. And say, "You just watch." I would razz her that she didn't have a face for T.V. only for radio. I mean, it rained heavily on us when we were walking from school one day and she did not get wet. That's how not good looking she was. The rain wouldn't even touch her. I know, I was a jerk growing up. She was no angel either and would call me the nastiest things ever. One day while sitting in my prison cell I saw her on T.V. I was blown away. I bragged to all the other inmates that I knew her, that we grew up together and were basically related. She was drop dead gorgeous. She was Beauuuttttiiffffuulll. I stalked her …no, wait, I tracked her and got her information, and we corresponded as friends. We talked about recovery and our past. She had ten years sober when we reacquainted, and she explained her freedom from addiction through taking the fourth step. She recounted her story to me.

All these years I was carrying guilt and shame that was not mine to bear. What was done to me as a child was not my fault. I was powerless over the violator of my youth. I was innocent. I am only responsible for how I reacted to the bad experience, though it left me feeling unworthy of love and needing to be validated by men. I was always needing to be rescued by some white knight. I reacted to my experiences by allowing my princess mentality of needing to be saved, control my life and make me codependent on a man. I couldn't see myself alone and always needed a man on "standby" in case my current relationship failed. If I didn't have a man on standby I wouldn't be single for very long.

It's embarrassing but when she was explaining things that were occurring to her because of traumatic experiences in life, I was feeling the same way and going through the same things. Not being single for long. Desperately longing for someone to love me instead of loving myself. Even though our experiences were not exactly the same. I could relate. There was something that felt so special and entrancing about our conversation that I felt it was divine. It was sensational. I was falling like I do because of that desperate longing as a loner has. I took the time to make the amends to her that I needed to make. I poured my heart out in apology. Begged her forgiveness. She brushed it off as just childhood banter and forgave me. She teased me about having a crush on her when we were children, and although I didn't have one then, I did now. I asked her out with thoughts of marriage and everything already speed racing in the back of my head and she just laughed. Then in all seriousness she said, "I always thought of you as ugly, and even if I were desperate and lonely you wouldn't be one of the men on a really long list I'd think of." haha. I guess I deserved that.

CHAPTER EIGHTEEN

    I want you to know I am not trying to promote anything. I'm not in recovery marketing and advertising in any way. I am not being paid to say this by some sponsored program nor am I endorsed by recovery programs of any kind. In fact, I hate how our world has become a sales sheep audience for ads and telemarketers which try to lure you to claim a prize or sign up for a subscription. I do hope that I may be able to fund my own recovery center someday. I do wish to have a farm that produces the crops I use for natural healing products. I strongly believe that recovery of the body and mind should go hand-in-hand. I would love to be remembered for carrying the message. Even if it's a crazy psychotic, sociopathic, traumatic spiritual way. One of the most complimentary things a friend, Terry Brown, said to me was, "You're like a spiritual gangster." I guess it fits.

    My sole purpose for writing this book is that I may help someone through the confusion and clouds of storms that I've lived through. I might help someone who struggled like me. I believe if I can make it anyone else can. I've managed to go from the wild and crazy life of chaos to the peace of God in recovery and sobriety. My being alive is testimony enough. My speaking on God and the great power of change is testament enough. I don't need to sell no one on that. If you know me, you know my life before God was absolute evil. And by absolute, I mean pure vodka was my blood type. I can tell you that recovery in a 12-step program works.

    The program of Alcoholics Anonymous has been the longest surviving free program that has turned out more sober people than all the recovery centers in the world combined. I strongly believe that this program can work for you as it did for millions of others. I don't believe this is the only avenue to finding God and getting sober. My Dad did it in a church. My book is based on the 12-step recovery program because this is the road in which my journey took me and I have tried everything, even that unwanted shock therapy in the beginning of my story. I do talk about the fourth step because I commonly hear the fears of "doing a moral inventory and then moving on to confessing to God, to themselves, and another human being the exact nature of their wrongs."

    Fortunately for me, in this case, my criminal defense attorney was my sponsor. Yes, my lawyer sponsored me. Yup. Twelve-stepped me in jail when I was on my way back for possession of ammunition and threatening a witness. He kicked me the Big Book and I laughed. I looked him straight in the eyes and told him, "You're kidding, right? It's not for me." Besides, I didn't want to read some spiritual book in jail. I was in the middle of reading a Danielle Steele Romance novel and I was just getting to the exciting parts. Spiritual readers were in the God-pod and that pod is for weirdos. For whatever reason though, I took the Big

Book up to the cell with me.

That night I couldn't sleep. There was an unsettling feeling deep down inside my soul. The thought of being sober never crossed my mind all my life, but the promise that I could be sober someday was fascinating to me. Imagine that. In the middle of the night, when they called lights out, I got up after being agitated enough, and started reading the Big Book. I sat by my cell door where a tiny light from the outside ceiling beamed through the window. I voraciously consumed the pages like my life depended on it. I memorized "How it works."

I remember being so immersed in this book that the feeling I've always had of comfort and peace washed over me like a tsunami and knocked me down like getting slammed by a 50-foot wave. Without even realizing it, I cried. I cried so many tears I could have drowned myself in my cell. I cried so many tears that I probably could have watered a prison garden. Even knowing all that, when my lawyer got me out, I went and drank. I painted the town blue that night and woke up to being sought out by the sheriffs for assaulting two people at the bar. I finally called my lawyer and said, "Hey, how does this thing really work? and I don't want the paper version." I wanted to really be sober.

Through the reluctance and fear, I went to visit my lawyer and he took me to my first meeting. It was most needed for both of us because his girlfriend was excited to hear he was going to one. Like I said, those we love know when we need one quicker than we do. From then things started to change in my life, drastically. Other people might have had suggestions to do the steps, but I was forced. My sponsor said, if you want me to help you change, I will go to hell with you. If you don't want to help me, help you, then you can go to hell by yourself. Forced. My sponsor even had me redo the fourth step three times before he was satisfied with me doing it. He had me come to his office where he gave me a legal pad in his office to get started on it and when I handed him back the legal pad with my fourth step he said BS. Do it again. My fourth step consisted of aliens and other things I blamed like my parents. When it was time to do the fifth step, I took out a dollar and gave it to my lawyer. Emphasis on LAWYER. I told my lawyer that it was a retainer.

If I was going to do this confessional with him then I would need to do it under the "Attorney/Client Privilege" act because I needed strict confidentiality. I didn't want anything I said coming back to haunt me legally like they've been doing spiritually for decades. I needed to know deep down that there wasn't going to be any legal ramifications afterwards. There was no other way I would've said anything to another living soul. As soon as he agreed, I poured into him from that minute on. I poured so deep from the nastiest and filthiest junk parts of my soul that after two hours I was emotionally spent and physically exhausted. I was so mentally and spiritually drained that I went home, prayed, and slept for three days straight like I was coming off a drinking binge. When I called and spoke to my lawyer later, he said he's happy I finally slept but he couldn't sleep a wink for those last three days.

Before I end this off, I want to remain faithful to God in my program. I need to stress this fact. The Big Book lays out the outline with the essential elements for a strong spiritual recovery. It's not a religious program of any sort. It is a spiritual one. If you are climbing out of that hell hole of a hospital for the spiritually sick, welcome home. We have a chair for you if you are wanting to get sober and change. We have people that are ready to help you find a God of your understanding by giving you the basics tools to develop this. We have people that can help you enhance and refine your spirituality if you are already there. Regardless of what program you get involved with, I believe the spiritual element is vital in recovery and to maintaining freedom. I know there are many programs out there that provide knowledge and tools to the alcoholics and addicts and plant the seeds of recovery in them, yet neglect teaching spirituality.

The difference between these programs and a spiritual one is simple. I can get out of prison with a head full of knowledge and tools in recovery, fear the repercussions and consequences, and still relapse or commit crimes; whereas with a spiritual program, I can get out and not have the greed that makes me steal. Not have the hate that makes me kill. Or not have the evil that makes me not know any better.

I believe that our nation is in a state where we need recovery now more than ever. Recovery in a mental, emotional, spiritual, and a physical sense. I have lost six people close to me, in the year of writing this book, to alcohol/substance abuse related deaths. With overdoses at an all-time high, I believe spreading the message can help us stem this climb in death tolls. I believe the truth is a rare find these days.

I write this book for the people that I recently lost.

I write this book for those that are struggling in the fight against this disease and are watching their close friends and comrades' relapse and die.

I write for those that have lost their voice, choked by a relapse they can't bring themselves back from.

I write this for my sons and daughter so that they may know the battles I've fought to get back to them.

I write most importantly for the victims of my drinking episodes. One of which lost his life in a savage beating death in a case the news called a 'mistaken identity.' I may not be able to bring him back. I may never be able to give his family what they want. Still, I can do my best to make sure that this thing never happens to someone else and honor him through this book on recovery.

I can do my part in helping others find a second chance to change and raise the awareness about alcohol abuse. I have learned in prison that time is the most valuable thing you have on Earth, that you should spend it wisely. I wish you well on your recovery. God bless you and thank you.

I want to end this book with a story that was told to me throughout my journey through recovery.

In a small village there lived the same wise old man and little boy. The wise old man was known for providing people with great counsel and he was who the village people went to for guidance and advice. One day, the boy decided he would confront the old man with a question that he knew the old man would not be able to answer correctly. His plan was to find a little bird and hold it cupped in his hands, hidden from sight. He would then approach the wise old man and ask him to guess what he had buried in his hands. If the old man answered it correctly, he would then ask him whether the bird was alive or dead? If the old man said the bird was alive, the boy would crush the bird with his hands and kill it, proving the wise old man wrong. But if the wise old man said it was dead, the boy would open his hands and let the bird fly free, demonstrating at last that the old man was not as wise as everyone thought him to be.

So, the boy ventured off and found a little sparrow that fit neatly within his hands. As he approached the old man, the boy said, "Old wise man, can you tell what I have in my hands?"

"Why, of course I can," the old man responded without hesitation. "From all the small feathers clinging to your jacket and the sound of chirping, I say you have a little bird cupped in your hands."

"Ah, that is so," the young boy exclaimed, "but is the bird alive or dead?"

The old man paused for a moment then rubbed his chin in contemplation of his response. The boy repeated, "So, is the bird alive or dead?"

Looking the young boy in the eyes, the old man replied in a soft tone, "Whether the bird is alive or dead is in your hand, my child. The choice is yours."

12 Steps of Alcoholics Anonymous from The Big Book

1. We admitted we were powerless over alcohol—that our lives had become unmanageable.
2. Came to believe that a Power greater than ourselves could restore us to sanity.
3. Made a decision to turn our will and our lives over to the care of God as we understood Him.
4. Made a searching and fearless moral inventory of ourselves.
5. Admitted to God, to ourselves, and to another human being the exact nature of our wrongs.
6. Were entirely ready to have God remove all these defects of character.
7. Humbly asked Him to remove our shortcomings.
8. Made a list of all persons we had harmed, and became willing to make amends to them all.
9. Made direct amends to such people wherever possible, except when to do so would injure them or others.
10. Continued to take personal inventory and when we were wrong promptly admitted it.
11. Sought through prayer and meditation to improve our conscious contact with God, as we understood Him, praying only for knowledge of His will for us and the power to carry that out.
12. Having had a spiritual awakening as the result of these Steps, we tried to carry this message to alcoholics, and to practice these principles in all our affairs.

APPENDIX

This is the dog that took us down.

Indictment Alleges "Violence, Murder, Bribery" and Federal Tax Dollars Used to Expand one of the Nation's Most Powerful Prison Gangs

By **Malia Zimmerman** - September 25, 2013

Kenneth Hines, IRS; Vida Bottom, FBI, Florence Nakakuni, US Attorney, Louis Kealoha, HPD and Max Otani, Public Safety Dept, announce major indictment of USO gang members and one former prison guard

This is the first indictment in a string of indictments that led to me being prosecuted for things I did prior to getting sober again. The next page details parts of my involvement in the conspiracy.

the above mention crystal methamphetamine and the delivery was intended for an individual named Patrick Prescott. The CI agreed to cooperate and participate in a controlled delivery.

2. On September 14, 2013, a Priority Mail parcel was intercepted by USPIS in Honolulu and opened via a federal search warrant. Discovered inside the Priority Mail parcel was approximately nine pounds of crystal methamphetamine. On September 16, 2013, a control delivery of the Priority Mail parcel was conducted and three suspects were arrested in relation to the control delivery. On September 21, 2013, a proffer was conducted with a cooperating defendant from the control delivery who stated he/she was a member of a street gang, Sons of Samoa and was being paid by Patrick Prescott to distribute narcotics. The cooperating defendant stated Patrick Prescott made the arrangements for narcotics being sent to Hawaii from the United States mainland. Furthermore, the cooperating defendant said he/she personally was involved with three separate packages of crystal methamphetamine being sent to Hawaii from the United States mainland. The cooperating defendant also stated he/she believed that some of the packages were being sent from the Seattle, Washington area. The cooperating defendant said the first package contained approximately five to six pounds of crystal methamphetamine and a second package contained 10 to 12 pounds of crystal methamphetamine. The cooperating defendant also said Patrick Prescott was in charge of the Drug Trafficking Organization in Hawaii. Patrick Prescott is currently incarcerated and is associated with a prison gang called "United Samoan Organization" (USO)

A. Seizure of $42,000 in United States Currency and Subsequent Investigation

3. On December 4, 2013 HSI in Honolulu, Hawaii intercepted a Priority Mail parcel sent from Guam to "Prescott Manisula" at "8402 East Sherwood Street, Tacoma, WA 98445". HSI executed a customs search of the parcel and discovered $42,000 in United States Currency (USC) in the parcel. HSI utilized a narcotics detection K9 which indicated a positive alert to the $42,000 in USC. The recipient of the package is believed to be Manisela Prescott. Moreover, agents believe Manisela Prescott is a relative of Patrick Prescott the indicated head of a Drug Trafficking Organization in Hawaii sending and receiving crystal methamphetamine via the U.S. Mail. According to Hawaii Criminal Justice Inquiry Patrick Prescott lists his address of record as 8402 E. Sherwood Street, Tacoma, WA 98444, virtually the same address to which the $42,000 USC was sent.

OFFICIAL USE ONLY

DEPARTMENT OF HOMELAND SECURITY ICE	PAGE 3
REPORT OF INVESTIGATION CONTINUATION	CASE NUMBER SE02PR14HL0006
	REPORT NUMBER: 009

DETAILES OF INVESTIGATION

On February 25, 2014, HSI Special Agent Joseph Abrew, USPIS Brett Willyerd, DEA TFO's Nick Jensen and Travis Kenyon debriefed a CI at the DEA office in Tacoma, Washington.

According to the CI, he/she was "working" for a Hispanic male named Oscar RODRIGUEZ-RODRIGUEZ. The CI said about four to five months ago, RODRIGUEZ-RODRIGUEZ arrived in the Tacoma area and has been providing methamphetamine to a Samoan male whom they called "Uncle Sam" The CI said RODRIGUEZ-RODRIGUEZ was supplying "Uncle Sam" with approximately 30 to 50 kilograms of methamphetamine per month. The CI said RODRIGUEZ-RODRIGUEZ told him/her that "Uncle Sam" was sending the methamphetamine to Hawaii through the U.S. mail. The CI also said RODRIGUEZ-RODRIGUEZ told him/her that a few times during the summer of 2013, RODRIGUEZ-RODRIGUEZ flew to Hawaii with "Uncle Sam" to pick up money from Hawaii to bring back to Washington State.

The CI also said in November 2013, he/she helped RODRIGUEZ-RODRIGUEZ count money that was given to RODRIGUEZ-RODRIGUEZ by "Uncle Sam". The CI said it was out $38,000.00. The CI said RODRIGUEZ-RODRIGUEZ only dealt with one Samoan. The CI said RODRIGUEZ-RODRIGUEZ told him/her that "Uncle Sam" was very heavy set and very tall. During a previous debrief, TFO Nick Jensen showed the CI a driver's license photograph of Manisela PRESCOTT. The CI said he/she saw PRESCOTT about a year ago at a party in Centralia, Washington. The CI said he/she recognized PRESCOTT in the driver's license photo because of the streak of white hair PRESCOTT had near his forehead. The CI also said PRESCOTT was the only Samoan at the party and that PRESCOTT came to the party with an individual named "Acapoquito" later identified as Gilberto VILLANUEVA-LEAL.

The CI did not think PRESCOTT was the same Samoan that RODRIGUEZ-RODRIGUEZ was supplying methamphetamine to because RODRIGUEZ-RODRIGUEZ described "Uncle Sam" as being very "fat". SA Abrew showed the CI a recent surveillance photograph of PRESCOTT. The CI said PRESCOTT looked a lot heavier than when he/she saw him about a year ago and that it was possible PRESCOTT is the Samoan that RODRIGUEZ-RODRIGUEZ was supplying the methamphetamine to.

The CI also said prior to RODRIGUEZ-RODRIGUEZ supplying methamphetamine to "Uncle Sam" there was an individual named "Caballo", later identified as Isidro BENITEZ-CASTILLO who was the main supplier of methamphetamine for "Uncle Sam". The CI said BENITEZ-CASTILLO was arrested in Portland and was deported back to Mexico but was now back in the Seattle/Tacoma area. The CI said BENITEZ-CASTILLO is running the methamphetamine trafficking operation now but has allowed RODRIGUEZ-RODRIGUEZ to continue supplying "Uncle Sam" with

OFFICIAL USE ONLY
IS DOCUMENT IS LOANED TO YOU FOR OFFICIAL USE ONLY AND REMAINS THE PROPERTY OF THE DEPARTMENT OF HOMELAND SECURITY, ICE. ANY FURTHER REQUEST FOR DISCLOSURE OF THIS DOCUMENT OR INFORMATION CONTAINED HEREIN SHOULD BE REFERRED TO ICE HEADQUARTERS TOGETHER WITH A COPY OF THE DOCUMENT.

OFFICIAL USE ONLY

DEPARTMENT OF HOMELAND SECURITY ICE	PAGE 4
REPORT OF INVESTIGATION CONTINUATION	CASE NUMBER SE02PR14HL0006
	REPORT NUMBER: 009

...hamphetamine.

The CI said sometime last week "Uncle Sam" ordered about six kilograms of methamphetamine from RODRIGUEZ-RODRIGUEZ. The CI said last week a shipment of liquid methamphetamine was transported to Tacoma from Arizona in a Ford F250 pickup truck. The CI said once the liquid methamphetamine was converted into a solid form, RODRIGUEZ-RODRIGUEZ would deliver the six kilograms of methamphetamine to "Uncle Sam". The CI said RODRIGUEZ-RODRIGUEZ had enough liquid methamphetamine to make 40 kilograms of solid methamphetamine.

The CI said RODRIGUEZ-RODRIGUEZ and BENITEZ-CASTILLO were expecting another shipment of liquid methamphetamine to be delivered to Tacoma sometime during the first week of March. The CI said the next shipment of liquid methamphetamine would be enough to make approximately 90 kilograms of methamphetamine in the solid form.

Investigation Continues

OFFICIAL USE ONLY
THIS DOCUMENT IS LOANED TO YOU FOR OFFICIAL USE ONLY AND REMAINS THE PROPERTY THE DEPARTMENT OF HOMELAND SECURITY, ICE. ANY FURTHER REQUEST FOR DISCLOSURE OF THIS DOCUMENT OR INFORMATION CONTAINED HEREIN SHOULD BE REFERRED TO ICE HEADQUARTERS TOGETHER WITH A COPY OF THE DOCUMENT.

Feds couldn't positively ID me through people that turned, and still felt the need to prosecute me.

AO 245B (Rev. 09/15) Judgment in a Criminal Case
Attachment (Page 2) — Statement of Reasons

Not for Public Disclosure

DEFENDANT: Manisela Prescott
CASE NUMBER: 3:14CR05526BHS-001
DISTRICT: Western District of Washington

STATEMENT OF REASONS

IV. GUIDELINE SENTENCING DETERMINATION *(Check all that apply)*

A. ☒ The sentence is within the guideline range and the difference between the maximum and minimum of the guideline range does not exceed 24 months.

B. ☐ The sentence is within the guideline range and the difference between the maximum and minimum of the guideline range exceeds 24 months, and the specific sentence is imposed for these reasons: *(Use Section VIII if necessary)*

C. ☐ The court departs from the guideline range for one or more reasons provided in the Guidelines Manual. *(Also complete Section V)*

D. ☐ The court imposed a sentence otherwise outside the sentencing guideline system (i.e., a variance). *(Also complete Section VI)*

V. DEPARTURES PURSUANT TO THE GUIDELINES MANUAL *(If applicable)*

A. **The sentence imposed departs:** *(Check only one)*
   ☐ above the guideline range
   ☐ below the guideline range

B. **Motion for departure before the court pursuant to:** *(Check all that apply and specify reason(s) in sections C and D)*
   1. **Plea Agreement**
      ☐ binding plea agreement for departure accepted by the court
      ☐ plea agreement for departure, which the court finds to be reasonable
      ☐ plea agreement that states that the government will not oppose a defense departure motion
   2. **Motion Not Addressed in a Plea Agreement**
      ☐ government motion for departure
      ☐ defense motion for departure to which the government did not object
      ☐ defense motion for departure to which the government objected
      ☐ joint motion by both parties
   3. **Other**
      ☐ Other than a plea agreement or motion by the parties for departure

C. **Reasons for departure:** *(Check all that apply)*

☐ 4A1.3	Criminal History Inadequacy	☐ 5K2.1	Death	☐ 5K2.12	Coercion and Duress
☐ 5H1.1	Age	☐ 5K2.2	Physical Injury	☐ 5K2.13	Diminished Capacity
☐ 5H1.2	Education and Vocational Skills	☐ 5K2.3	Extreme Psychological Injury	☐ 5K2.14	Public Welfare
☐ 5H1.3	Mental and Emotional Condition	☐ 5K2.4	Abduction or Unlawful Restraint	☐ 5K2.16	Voluntary Disclosure of Offense
☐ 5H1.4	Physical Condition	☐ 5K2.5	Property Damage or Loss	☐ 5K2.17	High-Capacity Semiautomatic Weapon
☐ 5H1.5	Employment Record	☐ 5K2.6	Weapon	☐ 5K2.18	Violent Street Gang
☐ 5H1.6	Family Ties and Responsibilities	☐ 5K2.7	Disruption of Government Function	☐ 5K2.20	Aberrant Behavior
☐ 5H1.11	Military Service	☐ 5K2.8	Extreme Conduct	☐ 5K2.21	Dismissed and Uncharged Conduct
☐ 5H1.11	Charitable Service/Good Works	☐ 5K2.9	Criminal Purpose	☐ 5K2.22	Sex Offender Characteristics
☐ 5K1.1	Substantial Assistance	☐ 5K2.10	Victim's Conduct	☐ 5K2.23	Discharged Terms of Imprisonment
☐ 5K2.0	Aggravating/Mitigating Circumstances	☐ 5K2.11	Lesser Harm	☐ 5K2.24	Unauthorized Insignia
				☐ 5K3.1	Early Disposition Program (EDP)

☐ Other Guideline Reason(s) for Departure, to include departures pursuant to the commentary in the Guidelines Manual:
(see "List of Departure Provisions" following the Index in the Guidelines Manual.) (Please specify)

D. **State the basis for the departure.** *(Use Section VIII if necessary)*

With the Feds, if you have downward departures in your paperwork, it shows you cooperated. I REFUSED to help the law take down friends I loved and grew up with, but that's not the case or these said friends. Many turned!

AO 245B   (Rev. 09/15) Judgment in a Criminal Case
          Attachment (Page 1) — Statement of Reasons

DEFENDANT: Manisela Prescott
CASE NUMBER: 3:14CR05526BHS-001
DISTRICT: Western District of Washington

STATEMENT OF REASONS
(Not for Public Disclosure)

Sections I, II, III, IV, and VII of the Statement of Reasons form must be completed in all felony and Class A misdemeanor cases.

I. COURT FINDINGS ON PRESENTENCE INVESTIGATION REPORT

A. ☐ The court adopts the presentence investigation report without change.

B. ☒ The court adopts the presentence investigation report with the following changes: *(Use Section VIII if necessary)*
   (Check all that apply and specify court determination, findings, or comments, referencing paragraph numbers in the presentence report)

   1. ☒ **Chapter Two of the United States Sentencing Commission Guidelines Manual** determinations by court:
      (briefly summarize the changes, including changes to base offense level, or specific offense characteristics)
      Court found base offense level to be 30, pursuant to U.S.S.G. § 2D1.1(c)(5), as agreed upon in Plea Agreement.

   2. ☐ **Chapter Three of the United States Sentencing Commission Guidelines Manual** determinations by court:

   3. ☐ **Chapter Four of the United States Sentencing Commission Guidelines Manual** determinations by court:
      (briefly summarize the changes, including changes to criminal history category or scores, career offender status, or criminal livelihood determinations)

   4. ☐ **Additional Comments or Findings:** *(include comments or factual findings concerning any information in the presentence report, including information that the Federal Bureau of Prisons may rely on when it makes inmate classification, designation, or programming decisions; any other rulings on disputed portions of the presentence investigation report; identification of those portions of the report in dispute but for which a court determination is unnecessary because the matter will not affect sentencing or the court will not consider it)*

C. ☐ The record establishes no need for a presentence investigation report pursuant to Fed.R.Crim.P. 32.

Applicable Sentencing Guideline: *(If more than one guideline applies, list the guideline producing the highest offense level)*

II. COURT FINDINGS ON MANDATORY MINIMUM SENTENCE *(Check all that apply)*

A. ☒ One or more counts of conviction carry a mandatory minimum term of imprisonment and the sentence imposed is at or above the applicable mandatory minimum term.

B. ☐ One or more counts of conviction carry a mandatory minimum term of imprisonment, but the sentence imposed is below the mandatory minimum term because the court has determined that the mandatory minimum term does not apply based on:
   ☐ findings of fact in this case: *(Specify)*
   _____
   ☐ substantial assistance *(18 U.S.C. § 3553(e))*
   ☐ the statutory safety valve *(18 U.S.C. § 3553(f))*

C. ☐ No count of conviction carries a mandatory minimum sentence.

III. COURT DETERMINATION OF GUIDELINE RANGE: *(BEFORE DEPARTURES OR VARIANCES)*

Total Offense Level: __27__
Criminal History Category: __IV__
Guideline Range: *(after application of §5G1.1 and §5G1.2)*   __120__ to __125__ months
Supervised Release Range: _____ to __5__ years
Fine Range: $ __12,500__ to $ __10,000,000__

☒ Fine waived or below the guideline range because of inability to pay.

www.ingramcontent.com/pod-product-compliance
Lightning Source LLC
Chambersburg PA
CBHW060321050426
42449CB00011B/2595